Maths minutes

100 minutes to practise and reinforce essential skills

Minute 4

Date: ....

Name: ....

Use the pictograph to complete Questions 1 and 2.

	Shapes found
Circle	○○○○○
Triangle	△△
Square	□□□□

1. Which shape was found most often? ....

2. How many squares were found?
   .... squares

3. Write the missing number in the pattern.
   ...., 12, 14

4. ...... the digit in the **hundreds** place.   345

5. ......ane has 3 toy cars. Liam has 7 toy cars.
   How many toy cars do they have altogether? .... cars

6. Look at the shaded figure. Circle the figure that is the same size and shape.

   ⬡   [A]   [B]   [C]   [D]

Use the number line to complete Questions 7 to 10.

0 1 2 3 4 5 6 7 8 9 10 11 12 13 14 15 16 17 18

7. $5 + 6 =$ ....

8. $4 + 9 =$ ....

9. $8 + 3 =$ ....

10. $7 + 5 =$ ....

My time: .... minutes .... seconds

My score: **10**

Maths minutes

④

Alaska Hults

6079UK

Maths minutes *Book 3*

Published by Prim-Ed Publishing® 2011 under licence to
Creative Teaching Press.
Copyright© 2005 Creative Teaching Press.
This version copyright© Prim-Ed Publishing® 2011

ISBN 978-1-84654-290-9
PR–6079

Titles available in this series:

Maths minutes – Book 1 *(Ages 5–6)*
Maths minutes – Book 2 *(Ages 6–7)*
Maths minutes – Book 3 *(Ages 7–8)*
Maths minutes – Book 4 *(Ages 8–9)*
Maths minutes – Book 5 *(Ages 9–10)*
Maths minutes – Book 6 *(Ages 10–11)*

Internet websites

In some cases, websites or specific URLs may be recommended. While these are checked and rechecked at the time of publication, the publisher has no control over any subsequent changes which may be made to webpages. It is *strongly* recommended that the class teacher checks *all* URLs before allowing pupils to access them.

View all pages online

Website: www.prim-ed.com

MATHS MINUTES – BOOK 3

Foreword

Maths minutes is a six-book series for pupils in primary schools that provides a structured daily programme of easy-to-follow activities in the mathematics areas of: **number, algebra, shape and space, measurement** and **handling data.**

The programme provides a framework to:

- *promote the ongoing learning of essential maths concepts and skills through practice and reinforcement*
- *develop and maintain speed of recall and maths fluency*
- *develop knowledge and understanding of mathematics terminology*
- *encourage mental maths strategies*
- *provide support to the overall daily mathematics programme.*

Maths minutes – Book 3 features 100 'minutes', each with 10 classroom-tested problems. The problems provide the pupils with practice in the key areas of mathematics for their year level, and basic computational skills. Designed to be implemented in numerical order from 1 to 100, the activities in *Maths minutes* are developmental through each book and across the series.

Comprehensive teachers notes, record-keeping charts, a scope-and-sequence table (showing when each new concept and skill is introduced), and photocopiable pupil reference materials are also included.

How many minutes does it take to complete a 'maths minute'?

Pupils will enjoy challenging themselves as they apply their mathematical knowledge and understanding to complete a 'maths minute' in the fastest possible time.

Titles available in this series:	**Age levels**
• *Maths minutes – Book 1*	Age 5–6 years
• *Maths minutes – Book 2*	Age 6–7 years
• *Maths minutes – Book 3*	Age 7–8 years
• *Maths minutes – Book 4*	Age 8–9 years
• *Maths minutes – Book 5*	Age 9–10 years
• *Maths minutes – Book 6*	Age 10–11 years

Contents

Teachers notes

How to use this book

Maths minutes can be used in a variety of ways, such as:

- **a speed test.** As the teacher starts a stopwatch, pupils begin the 'minute'. As each pupil finishes, he/she raises a hand and the teacher calls out the time. The pupil records this time on the appropriate place on the sheet. Alternatively, a particular time can be allocated for the whole class to complete the 'minute' in.

  Pupils record their scores and time on their 'minute journal' (see page vii).

- **a whole-class activity.** Work through the 'minute' together as a teaching or reviewing activity.

- **a warm-up activity.** Use a 'minute' a day as a 'starter' or warm-up activity before the main part of the maths lesson begins.

- **a homework activity.** If given as a homework activity, it would be most beneficial for the pupils if the 'minute' is corrected and reviewed at the start of the following lesson.

Maths minutes strategies

Encourage pupils to apply the following strategies to help improve their scores and decrease the time taken to complete the 10 questions.

- To use mental maths strategies whenever possible.
- To move quickly down the page, answering the problems they know first.
- To come back to problems they are unsure of, after they have completed all other problems.
- To make educated guesses when they encounter problems they are not familiar with.
- To rewrite word problems as number problems.

A *Maths minute* pupil activity page.

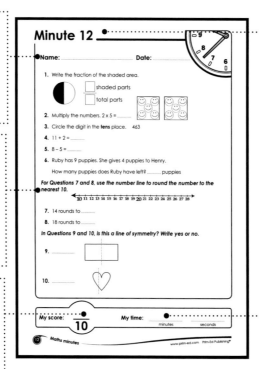

Name and date
Pupils write their name and the date in the spaces provided.

Questions
There are 10 problems, providing practice in every key area of the maths strands.

Score
Pupils record their score out of 10 in the space provided.

'Maths minute' number
Maths minutes are designed to be completed in numerical order.

Time
Pupils record the time taken to complete the 'minute' at the bottom of the sheet. (This is optional.)

 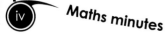

Teachers notes

Marking

Answers are provided for all activities. How these activities are marked will vary according to the teacher's organisational policy. Methods could include whole-class checking, partner checking, individual pupil checking, or collection by the teacher.

Diagnosis of problem areas

Maths minutes provides the teacher with immediate feedback of whole-class and individual pupil understanding. This information is useful for future programming and planning of further opportunities to practise and review the skills and concepts which need addressing.

Make use of the structured nature of the questions to diagnose problem areas; rather than asking who got 10 out of 10, ask the pupils who got Number 1 correct to raise their hands, Number 2, Number 3 etc. This way you will be able to quickly determine which concepts and calculations are causing problems for the majority of the pupils. Once the routine of *Maths minutes* is established, the teacher will have time to work with individuals or small groups to assist them with any areas causing problems.

Meeting the needs of individuals

The structure of *Maths minutes* allows some latitude in the way the books are used; for example, it may be impractical (as well as demoralising for some) for all pupils to be using the same book. It can also be difficult for teachers to manage the range of abilities found in any one classroom, so while pupils may be working at different levels from different books, the familiar structure makes it easier to cope with individual differences. An outline of the suggested age range levels of each book is suited to is given on page iii.

Additional resources:

- **Minute records**

  Teachers can record pupil scores and times on the **Minute records** table located on page vi.

- **Scope and sequence:**

  The **Scope-and-sequence table** gives the 'minute' in which each new skill and concept appears for the first time.

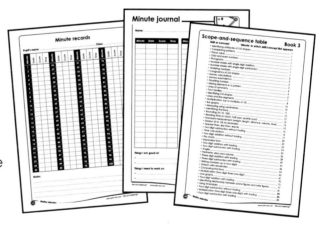

- **Minute journal**

  Once a 'minute' is completed, pupils record their score and time on their **Minute journal**, located on page vii.

- **Useful maths facts:**

  Two pages of photocopiable pupil reference materials have been included, which pupils can refer to when required.

- **Answers to all questions are found on pages 101 to 105.**

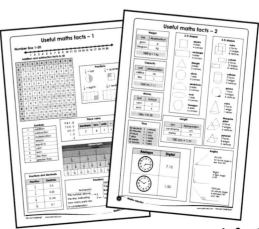

Minute records

Pupil's name: .... **Class:** ....

Minute:	Date	Score	Time	Minute:	Date	Score	Time	Minute:	Date	Score	Time	Minute:	Date	Score	Time
1				26				51				76			
2				27				52				77			
3				28				53				78			
4				29				54				79			
5				30				55				80			
6				31				56				81			
7				32				57				82			
8				33				58				83			
9				34				59				84			
10				35				60				85			
11				36				61				86			
12				37				62				87			
13				38				63				88			
14				39				64				89			
15				40				65				90			
16				41				66				91			
17				42				67				92			
18				43				68				93			
19				44				69				94			
20				45				70				95			
21				46				71				96			
22				47				72				97			
23				48				73				98			
24				49				74				99			
25				50				75				100			

Notes:

....

....

....

....

Minute journal

Name: ....

Minute	Date	Score	Time

Minute	Date	Score	Time

Things I am good at:

- ....
- ....

Things I need to work on:

- ....
- ....

Things I am good at:

- ....
- ....

Things I need to work on:

- ....
- ....

Scope-and-sequence table　　Book 3

Skill or concept　　　'Minute' in which skill/concept first appears

www.prim-ed.com　　Prim-Ed Publishing®

Useful maths facts – 1

Number line 1–20

$$\longleftarrow \bullet \; 1 \;\; 2 \;\; 3 \;\; 4 \;\; 5 \;\; 6 \;\; 7 \;\; 8 \;\; 9 \;\; 10 \;\; 11 \;\; 12 \;\; 13 \;\; 14 \;\; 15 \;\; 16 \;\; 17 \;\; 18 \;\; 19 \;\; 20 \; \longrightarrow$$

Addition and subtraction facts to 20

+	0	1	2	3	4	5	6	7	8	9	10
0	0	1	2	3	4	5	6	7	8	9	10
1	1	2	3	4	5	6	7	8	9	10	11
2	2	3	4	5	6	7	8	9	10	11	12
3	3	4	5	6	7	8	9	10	11	12	13
4	4	5	6	7	8	9	10	11	12	13	14
5	5	6	7	8	9	10	11	12	13	14	15
6	6	7	8	9	10	11	12	13	14	15	16
7	7	8	9	10	11	12	13	14	15	16	17
8	8	9	10	11	12	13	14	15	16	17	18
9	9	10	11	12	13	14	15	16	17	18	19
10	10	11	12	13	14	15	16	17	18	19	20

Fractions

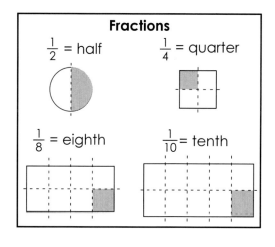

$\frac{1}{2}$ = half $\frac{1}{4}$ = quarter

$\frac{1}{8}$ = eighth $\frac{1}{10}$ = tenth

Symbols

+	addition
–	subtraction
×	multiplication
÷	division
=	equal to
p	pence
£	pound
<	less than
>	greater than

Place value

```
7 4 1 . 2
7 0 0 . 0
  4 0 . 0
    1 . 0
      . 2
```

hundreds	tens	units	•	tenths
7	4	1	•	2

Equivalent fractions
one whole

$\frac{1}{2}$				$\frac{1}{2}$			
$\frac{1}{4}$		$\frac{1}{4}$		$\frac{1}{4}$		$\frac{1}{4}$	
$\frac{1}{8}$	$\frac{1}{8}$	$\frac{1}{8}$	$\frac{1}{8}$	$\frac{1}{8}$	$\frac{1}{8}$	$\frac{1}{8}$	$\frac{1}{8}$
$\frac{1}{10}$	$\frac{1}{10}$	$\frac{1}{10}$	$\frac{1}{10}$	$\frac{1}{10}$	$\frac{1}{10}$	$\frac{1}{10}$	$\frac{1}{10}$	$\frac{1}{10}$	$\frac{1}{10}$

Fractions and decimals

Fraction	Decimal
$\frac{1}{2}$	0.5
$\frac{1}{4}$	0.25
$\frac{1}{8}$	0.125
$\frac{1}{10}$	0.1

Fractions

Numerator
The number above the line, indicating how many parts are in consideration.

Denominator
The number below the line, indicating how many parts the whole number is divided into.

$\frac{3}{4}$

Useful maths facts – 2

Weight

Unit	Abbreviation
gram	g
kilogram	kg

1000 g = 1 kg

Capacity

Unit	Abbreviation
millilitre	mL
litre	L

1000 mL = 1 L

Money

Unit	Symbol
pence	p
pound	£

100p = £1.00

Time

60 seconds	=	1 minute
60 minutes	=	1 hour
24 hours	=	1 day
7 days	=	1 week
52 weeks	=	1 year
12 months	=	1 year

Analogue	Digital
	7.15
	1.50

2-D shapes

square
4 sides
4 corners

rectangle
4 sides
4 corners

triangle
3 sides
3 corners

circle
1 side
0 corners

semicircle
2 sides
2 corners

oval
1 side
0 corners

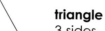
hexagon
6 sides
6 corners

Length

Unit	Abbreviation
centimetre	cm
metre	m

100 cm = 1 m

3-D shapes

cube
6 faces
12 edges
8 vertices

cuboid
6 faces
12 edges
8 vertices

cylinder
3 faces
2 edges
0 vertices

sphere
1 face
0 edges
0 vertices

cone
2 faces
1 edge
1 vertex

triangular prism
5 faces
9 edges
6 vertices

pyramid
5 faces
8 edges
5 vertices

Angles

Acute
An acute angle is less than 90°.

Right
A right angle is 90°.

Obtuse
An obtuse angle is between 90° and 180°.

www.prim-ed.com   Prim-Ed Publishing®

Minute 1

Name: .... Date: ....

1. Write the next number in the pattern.

   2, 4, 6, 8, ...

2. There are .... corners on the shape.

3. Is 11 an **odd** or **even** number? ....

4. Circle the digit in the **tens** place.　　264

5. There are 3 blue blocks and 5 red blocks.
   How many blocks are there altogether? .... blocks

6. Milo has 7 pencils. He gives 2 to a friend.
   How many pencils does Milo have left? .... pencils

Use the pictogram to complete Questions 7 and 8.

Favourite sport

Baseball	🏏 🏏
Football	⚽ ⚽ ⚽ ⚽
Swimming	🥽 🥽 🥽

(Each symbol equals one child.)

7. How many children like swimming? .... children

8. Which sport is most popular? ....

For Questions 9 and 10, write true or false.

9. 7 comes **after** 17. ....

10. 12 comes **before** 11. ....

My score: _____
10

My time: ....
　　　　　　minutes　　　seconds

Minute 2

Name: .... **Date:** ....

1. Look at the shaded figure. Circle the figure that is the same shape and size.

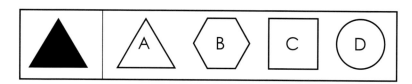

2. 6 + 3 = ...

3. Write the next number in the pattern.   0, 5, 10, 15, ...

4.  +   = ...p

5. Circle each group. Write how many are in each group.

   There are .... in each group.

6. Circle the digit in the **ones** place.   365

For Questions 7 and 8, circle the greater number.

7. 15   21

8. 45   39

Use the number line to complete Questions 9 and 10.

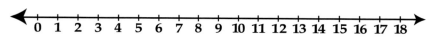

9. 12 – 2 = ...

10. 12 – 6 = ...

My score: ____ / **10**   **My time:** ....
                                              minutes   seconds

www.prim-ed.com   Prim-Ed Publishing®

Minute 3

Name: .... **Date:** ....

1. 100 pence = ... pound

2. Ed had 10 biscuits. He gave 3 to his teacher.

   How many biscuits does Ed have left? .... biscuits

3. Is 8 an **odd** or **even** number? ....

4. 4 + 3 = ...

5. 5 + 4 = ...

6. Emma picked 3 daisies and 5 roses.

   How many flowers did she pick altogether? .... flowers

For Questions 7 and 8, write true or false.

7. 40 is between 39 and 41. ....

8. 14 is between 41 and 50. ....

For Questions 9 and 10, complete the number sentence.

9. 3 + 3 = ...

10. 5 + 5 = ...

My score: _____ **My time:** ....
        10   minutes   seconds

Minute 4

Name: .... Date: ....

Use the pictogram to complete Questions 1 and 2.

Shapes found

Circle	○ ○ ○ ○ ○
Triangle	△ △
Square	□ □ □ □

1. Which shape was found most

often? ....

2. How many squares were found?

.... squares

3. Write the missing number in the pattern.

2, 4, 6, 8, ..., 12, 14

4. Circle the digit in the **hundreds** place.   345

5. Shane has 3 toy cars. Liam has 7 toy cars.

How many toy cars do they have altogether? .... cars

6. Look at the shaded figure. Circle the figure that is the same size and shape.

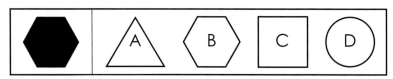

Use the number line to complete Questions 7 to 10.

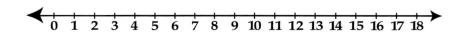

7. 5 + 6 = ...

8. 4 + 9 = ...

9. 8 + 3 = ...

10. 7 + 5 = ...

My score: $\dfrac{}{10}$ My time: ....
                                         minutes   seconds

Minute 5

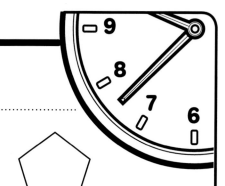

Name: .... **Date:** ....

1. There are .... corners on the shape.

2. Eli has 2 dogs. Anna has 5 dogs.

   Who has the **greater** number of dogs? ....

3. 3 + 6 = ...

4. Circle the picture that shows symmetry.

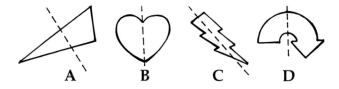

5. 5 – 4 = ...

6. 2 + 5 = ... + 2

7. Write the next number in the pattern.

   3, 6, 9, 12, ...

8. Write 7, 5 and 12 in order from **greatest** to **least**. ....

For Questions 9 and 10, write before, after **or** between **to complete the sentence.**

9. 7 comes .... 6 and 8.

10. 21 comes .... 31 and 41.

My score: ———
10

My time: ....
minutes   seconds

Minute 6

Name: .... **Date:** ....

1. Circle the name of the shape.

    circle   square   triangle   rectangle

2. Write the next number in the pattern.

    4, 8, 12, 16, ...

3. Will has a pair of skates. There are 4 wheels on each skate.

    How many wheels are there altogether? .... wheels

4. Circle the digit in the **tens** place.   426

5. How many corners are on the shape? .... corners

6. Complete the fact family.

    2 + 3 = 5   5 – 2 = 3

    3 + 2 = ...   5 – 3 = 2

Use the number line to complete Questions 7 to 10.

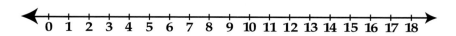

7. 15 – 4 = ...

8. 16 – 8 = ...

9. 14 – 7 = ...

10. 13 – 9 = ...

My score: $\dfrac{}{10}$ **My time:** ....
                                            minutes   seconds

www.prim-ed.com   Prim-Ed Publishing®

Minute 7

Name: .... **Date:** ....

1. Circle the name of the 3-D shape.

   cube   cylinder   sphere   pyramid

2. Erin has 3 fish. Each fish has 2 fins.

   How many fish fins are there altogether? .... fins

3. Circle the **difference**. $9 - 4 = 5$

4. Circle the **sum**. $9 + 4 = 13$

5. Circle the **odd** number.   3   8

6. Complete the fact family.

   $4 + 6 = 10$ $10 - 4 =$ ....

   $6 + 4 =$ .... $10 - 6 = 4$

7. $7 +$ .... $= 9$

For Questions 8 to 10, draw circles to show the sum of the doubles and complete the number sentence.

8. $+$ $=$ $2 + 2 =$ ....

9. $+$ $=$ $5 + 5 =$ ....

10. $+$ $=$ $7 + 7 =$ ....

My score: $\dfrac{\quad\quad}{10}$ **My time:** ....

                                                                minutes   seconds

Minute 8

Name: .... **Date:** ....

1. Circle the hexagon.

2. Circle the **even** number.

   3   8

3. Circle the open figures.

4. This is a line segment. Circle: True   or   False

5. 6 + 3 = ...

6. 9 – 2 = ...

7. 4 + 3 + 2 = ...

For Questions 8 to 10, write before, after **or** between **to complete the sentence.**

8. 7 comes .... 10 and 12.

9. 9 comes .... 8 and 12.

10. 14 comes .... 5 and 9.

My score: _____ /10

My time: ....
minutes   seconds

www.prim-ed.com   Prim-Ed Publishing®

Minute 9

Name: .... **Date:** ....

1. Kay has 6 pencils. Tran has 16 pencils.

   Who has more pencils? ....

2. Circle the name of the 3-D shape.

   cube   tetrahedron   cylinder   sphere

3. Write the **difference**. 12 − 6 = ...

4. Write the **sum**. 12 + 6 = ...

5. How many sides does the shape have? .... sides

6. Write the missing number in the pattern.

   5, 10, ..., 20, 25

Use the number line to complete Questions 7 to 10.

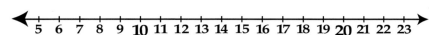

7. 9 + 6 = ...

8. 8 + 8 = ...

9. 9 + 9 = ...

10. 5 + 12 = ...

My score: $\dfrac{\quad}{10}$ **My time:** ....
                                                   minutes   seconds

Minute 10

Name: .... Date: ....

1. This line segment has two names. The names are .... and $\overleftrightarrow{DC}$.

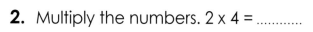

C ● ————————— ● D

2. Multiply the numbers. 2 x 4 = ...

3. 10 + 8 = ...

4. The coin is worth .... pence.

5. Complete the fact family.

    5 + 7 = 12   7 + 5 = ...

    12 – 7 = ...   12 – 5 = 7

6. Cara and Sam each have 2 yoyos.

   How many yoyos do they have altogether? .... yoyos

7. Natalie has 3 dogs. Tony has 5 dogs.

   Who has the greater number of dogs? ....

Use the bar graph to complete Questions 8 to 10.

8. Which drink is the

   most popular? ....

9. Which drink is the

   least popular? ....

10. Which two drinks were chosen by

    the same number of people?

    .... and ....

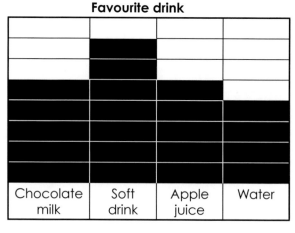

Favourite drink

My score: ———— / 10

My time: ....
              minutes   seconds

Minute 11

Name: .... **Date:** ....

1. Multiply the numbers. 2 x 3 = ...

2. Write 16, 9, 20, and 7 in order

    from **least** to **greatest**. ....

3. What is the **difference** between 8 and 6? ....

4. What is the **sum** of 8 and 6? ....

5. Complete the fact family.   7 + 8 = 15   8 + 7 = ...

    15 – 8 = ...   15 – 7 = 8

6. How long is AB? .... cm   A⎯⎯B

7. Nancy has 3 ten-pence pieces. Joe has 5 five-pence pieces.

    Who has the **greater** amount of money? ....

For Questions 8 to 10, circle the figure that is congruent (same shape and size) to the shaded figure.

8.

9.

10.   B C D

My score: _____
10

My time: ....
                    minutes   seconds

Minute 12

Name: .... **Date:** ....

1. Write the fraction of the shaded area.

$\dfrac{\boxed{}}{\boxed{}}$ shaded parts

total parts

2. Multiply the numbers. 2 x 5 = ...

3. Circle the digit in the **tens** place.   463

4. 11 + 2 = ...

5. 8 – 5 = ...

6. Ruby has 9 puppies. She gives 4 puppies to Henry.

   How many puppies does Ruby have left? .... puppies

For Questions 7 and 8, use the number line to round the number to the nearest 10.

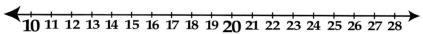

7. 14 rounds to ....

8. 18 rounds to ....

In Questions 9 and 10, is this a line of symmetry? Write yes or no.

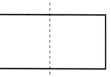

9. ....

10. ....

My score: $\dfrac{}{10}$ **My time:** ....

minutes   seconds

www.prim-ed.com Prim-Ed Publishing®

Minute 13

Name: .... Date: ....

1. Multiply the numbers. $3 \times 3 =$ ....

2. Write 32, 46 and 24 in order

   from **least** to **greatest**. ....

3. Write the missing number in the pattern.   5, 10, 15, ..., 25, 30

4. Complete the fact family. $8 + 3 = 11$ $3 + 8 =$ ....

                                 $11 - 8 =$ .... $11 - 3 = 8$

5. How long is this line? Circle the answer.

   |———————| 3 m   3 cm   3 mm

6. What time does the clock show?

   Quarter past .... or 15

7. $10 - 7 =$ ....

Use the bar graph to complete Questions 8 to 10.

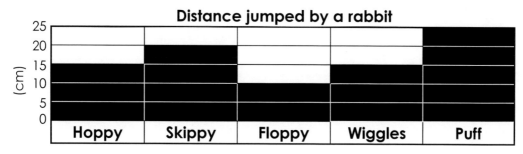

Distance jumped by a rabbit

8. Which rabbit jumped the farthest distance? ....

9. Which rabbit jumped the shortest distance? ....

10. Which two rabbits jumped an equal distance?

    .... and ....

My score: _____ **10**   My time: ....
                                         minutes   seconds

Minute 14

Name: .... **Date:** ....

1. 18 – 5 = ...

2. Multiply the numbers. 3 x 4 = ...

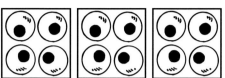

3. 12 + 4 = ...

4. Write 321, 776 and 335 in order from **least** to **greatest**. ....

5. Andy is selling lemonade for 50p a cup. Alice wants to buy one cup.

   Which coins should she give Andy? Circle the answer.

6. 20 + 10 = ...

For Questions 7 to 10, use the number line to round each number to the nearest ten.

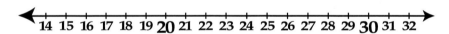

14 15 16 17 18 19 **20** 21 22 23 24 25 26 27 28 29 **30** 31 32

7. 24 rounds to ....

8. 18 rounds to ....

9. 27 rounds to ....

10. 19 rounds to ....

My score:

10

My time: ....
                        minutes   seconds

www.prim-ed.com   Prim-Ed Publishing®

Minute 15

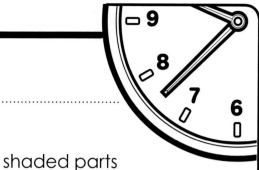

Name: .... Date: ....

1. Write the fraction of the shaded area. ☐ shaded parts / ☐ total parts

2. Multiply the numbers. 3 x 5 = ...

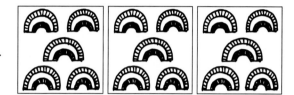

3.

   There are .... sets of two in 4.   4 ÷ 2 = ...

4. This line segment has two names. The names are .... and $\overrightarrow{BA}$.

   A   B

5. 3 + 2 + 2 = ...

6. Circle how many millimetres are in 1 centimetre.   1   10   100   1000

7. Is 10 odd or even? ....

8. How many days are in a fortnight? Circle the answer.   7   14   28

9. A triangle has .... sides.

10. 100 + 20 + 3 = ...

My score: _____ / 10   My time: ....
                                              minutes   seconds

Minute 16

Name: .... **Date:** ....

1. 7 + 2 + 0 = ...

2. Multiply the numbers. 4 x 2 = ...

3. 4 x 0 = ...

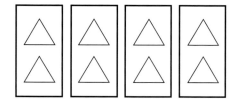

4. Circle the abbreviation for litre.   l   lt   L

5. Circle how many grams are in a kilogram.   10   100   1000

6. There are .... sets of two in 8.

       8 ÷ 2 = ...

7. There are .... sets of two in 6.

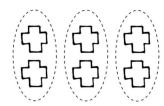

       6 ÷ 2 = ...

Use <, > or = to complete Questions 8 and 9.

8. 126 ☐ 261

9. 342 ☐ 231

10.   19
    – 4
    ....

    ....

My score: $\dfrac{}{10}$ **My time:** ....
                                                   minutes   seconds

www.prim-ed.com   Prim-Ed Publishing®

Minute 17

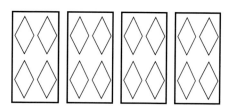

Name: .... **Date:** ....

1. 4 + 0 + 5 = ...

2. Multiply the numbers. 4 x 4 = ...

3. Circle the digit in the **hundreds** place. 529

4. A triangle has three angles and .... sides.

5. Dana has 50p. She earns another 25p by cleaning the dishes.

   How much money does she have altogether? ....

6.   28
      − 6
   ....

   ....

7. There are .... sets of two in 12.

   12 ÷ 2 = ...

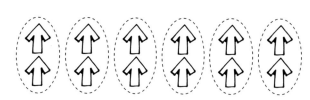

8. Lily read 3 books in June, 8 in July and 4 in August.

   How many books did she read altogether? .... books

For Questions 9 and 10, write how many minutes have passed.

9. 1.15 to 1.45 = ... minutes

10. 2.00 to 2.15 = ... minutes

My score: $\dfrac{\qquad}{10}$

My time: ....

....
minutes   seconds

Minute 18

Name: .... **Date:** ....

1. Circle the name of the shape.

   pentagon   hexagon   octagon

2. Write the fraction of the shaded area.

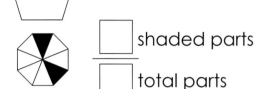

$\dfrac{}{}$ shaded parts / total parts

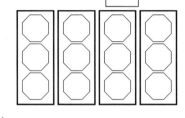

3. Multiply the numbers. 4 x 3 = ...

4. Write 142, 114 and 287 in order from

   least to **greatest**. ....

5. 5 + 1 + 4 = ...

6. Complete the fact family.   9 + 4 = 13   4 + 9 = ...

                                         13 – 4 = ...   13 – 9 = 4

7.   28
      –13
      ....

      ....

Use the bar graph to complete Questions 8 to 10.

8. Which ice-cream flavour is

   most popular? ....

9. Which ice-cream flavour is

   least popular? ....

10. How many more children preferred
    vanilla than preferred strawberry?

    .... more children

Favourite flavour of ice-cream

	Chocolate	Vanilla	Strawberry
7			
6			
5			
4			
3			
2			
1			
0			

My score: $\dfrac{}{10}$ **My time:** ....

                                             minutes   seconds

Minute 19

Name: .... Date: ....

1. £1.50 + £2.50 = ...

2. Write 308, 350 and 318 in order from **least** to **greatest**.

   ....

3. Circle the abbreviation for grams.   g   gms   G

4. 6 + 1 + 2 = ...

5. Multiply the numbers. 4 x 5 = ...

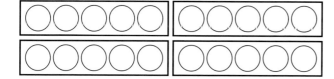

6. There are .... sets of two in 10.   10 ÷ 2 = ...

7. 10 millimetres = ... centimetre(s)

Use <, >, or = to complete Questions 8 to 10.

8. 1426 1326

9. 2510 3564

10. 1628 1638

My score: ────
10

My time: ....
              minutes   seconds

Minute 20

Name: .... **Date:** ....

1. There are .... sets of two in 14.

   $14 \div 2 =$ ....

   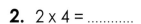

2. $2 \times 4 =$ ....

3. A pentagon has .... sides.

4. 63
   − 21
   ....

   ....

5. .... km = 1000 m

6. 14
   + 13
   ....

   ....

7. At the park, Sue counted 4 geese and 12 ducks.

   How many fewer geese than ducks were there? .... fewer geese

8. Which number is the product? .... $7 \times 6 = 42$

For Questions 9 and 10, circle the figure that is congruent (same shape and size) to the shaded figure.

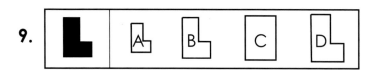

9.

10.

Minute 21

Name: .... Date: ....

1. 3 x 3 = ...

2. Write 42, 420, 242 and 24 in order from **least** to **greatest**.

   ....

3.   54
    − 33
    ....

    ....

4. A rectangle has four angles and .... sides.

5.   53
    + 10
    ....

    ....

6. Circle the abbreviation for metre.   m   mtr   M

7. 6 ÷ 3 = ...

8. Haley bought 14 jelly beans and 12 mints.

   How many sweets did she buy altogether? .... sweets

In Questions 9 and 10, is this a line of symmetry? Write yes or no.

9. ....

10. ....

My score: _____
         10

My time: ....
                minutes   seconds

Minute 22

Name: .... **Date:** ....

1. Write the fraction of the shaded area.

[ ] shaded parts

[ ] total parts

2. 9 ÷ 3 = ...

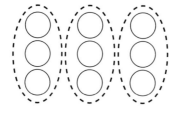

3. Circle the digit in the **ones** place. 921

4. A rectangle has .... angles and .... sides.

5.   65
       − 22
       ....

       ....

6. 1 metre = ... centimetres

7. £10.00 − £5.50 = ...

8. 1 litre = ... millilitres

9. 4 x 7 = ...

10.   26
       + 21
       ....

       ....

My score: _____
              10

My time: ....
            minutes   seconds

www.prim-ed.com   Prim-Ed Publishing®

Minute 23

Name: .... Date: ....

1. 12 ÷ 3 = ...

2. The expanded form of 237 is 200 + 30 + ...

3. Complete the fact family. 5 + 8 = ... 13 – 5 = ...

   8 + 5 = 13 13 – 8 = 5

4.   60
   + 39
   ....

   ....

5. What time does the clock show? 35

6. Write the next two numbers in the pattern.

   6, 12, 18, 24, 30, ..., ...

7. 3 x 9 = ...

Use the pie chart to complete Questions 8 to 10.

8. How do most pupils

   get to school? ....

9. What is the least common way pupils

   get to school? ....

10. How many more pupils walk to school

   than ride their bikes? .... more pupils

How pupils get to school

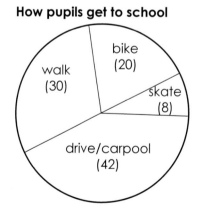

My score: _____
10

My time: ....
minutes seconds

Minute 24

Name: .... **Date:** ....

1. Ash had 14 lollipops. He gave 4 lollipops away to his friends.

   How many lollipops does he have left? .... lollipops

2. The expanded form of 253 is 200 + ... + 3.

3. Write the fraction of the shaded area.

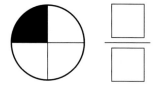

4. 3 x 8 = ...

5. 15 ÷ 3 = ...

6.   34
     + 17
     ....

     ....

7. 7 x 7 = 49   Which number is a **factor**? ....

For Questions 8 to 10, use the number line to round the number to the nearest ten.

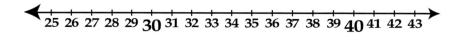

8. 36 rounds to ....

9. 28 rounds to ....

10. 35 rounds to ....

My score: $\dfrac{}{10}$ **My time:** ....
                                                minutes   seconds

Minute 25

Name: .... **Date:** ....

1. Circle the name of the 3-D shape.

sphere   cube   cylinder   pyramid

2.   25
   + 35
   ....

   ....

3. Multiply the numbers. 2 x 0 = ...

4.   63
   − 24
   ....

   ....

5. 30 + 40 = ...

6. 18 ÷ 3 = ...

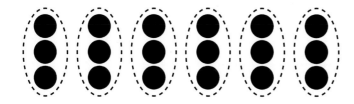

7. 4 x 6 = 24   Which number is the **product**? ....

8. 8 x 5 = 40   Which numbers are the **factors**? ....

9. A hexagon has .... sides.

10. Halve 50. ....

My score: $\frac{\qquad}{10}$ **My time:** ....
                                                         minutes   seconds

Minute 26

Name: .... Date: ....

1. 21 ÷ 3 = ...

2. This is an angle.

   Circle: True or False

3. 1 x 6 = ...

4. There are .... angles and .... sides on the shape.

5. 2 x 9 = ...

6.   86
   + 15
   ....

   ....

7. Write 910, 91, 19 and 901 in order from **least** to **greatest**.

   ....

8. The expanded form of 529 is .... + 20 + ...

For Questions 9 and 10, round the number to the nearest ten.

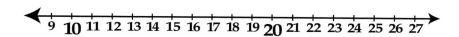

9. 14 rounds to ....

10. 18 rounds to ....

My score: _____ / 10   My time: .... minutes .... seconds

www.prim-ed.com   Prim-Ed Publishing®

Minute 27

Name: .... Date: ....

1. The expanded form of 921 is .... + ... + ...

2. $8 \div 4 =$ ....

3. Write the fraction of the shaded area.

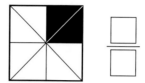

4. $6 \times 2 =$ ....

5. Brian has 50p. He mows the lawn and earns an additional £1.00.

   How much money does he have now? ....

6.

7.   44
     + 48
     ....

     ....

8. What is the abbreviation for **millilitre**? ....

In Questions 9 and 10, does the figure have symmetry? Circle Yes or No.

If yes, draw the line of symmetry.

9. Yes   No

10. Yes   No

Minute 28

Name: .... **Date:** ....

1. Circle the name of the shape. pentagon   hexagon   octagon

2. 1 pound = ... pence

3. 1 centimetre = ... millimetres

4. 16 ÷ 4 = ...

5. The perimeter of the shape is 9.

   Circle: True   or   False

6. 5 x 6 = ...

7.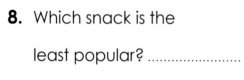
   ```
    36
   + 56
   ........

   ........
   ```

Use the bar graph to complete Questions 8 to 10.

8. Which snack is the

   least popular? ....

9. Which snack is the

   most popular? ....

10. Which two snacks are liked
    equally?

    ....

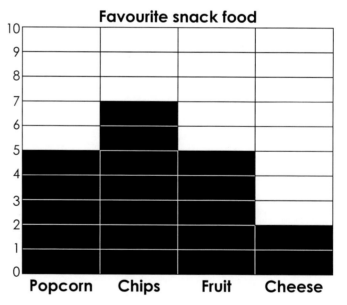

My score: $\dfrac{}{10}$ My time: ....
                                              minutes   seconds

www.prim-ed.com   Prim-Ed Publishing®

Name: .... **Date:** ....

1. 54
    + 28
    ....

    ....

2. The expanded form of 556 is .... + ... + ...

3. The perimeter of the shape is 12.

    Circle: True   or   False

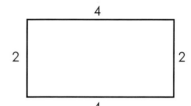

4. 24 ÷ 4 = ...

5. 7 x 2 = ...

6. 96
    − 35
    ....

    ....

7. 3)6̄

8. Circle the abbreviation for **kilogram.**   kg   klg   Kg

For Questions 9 and 10, write how much time has passed.

9. 3.15 to 3.45 = ... minutes

10. 4.00 to 4.45 = ... minutes

My score: ──────
              10

My time: ....
                    minutes   seconds

Minute 30

Name: .... **Date:** ....

1. 32 ÷ 4 = ...

2. 45 + 10 = ...

3. Write the fraction of the shaded area.

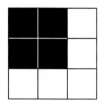

4. 5 x 6 = ...

5. The perimeter of the shape is 12.

Circle: True or False

6. 66
+ 37
....

....

7. The expanded form of 831 is .... + ... + ...

8. 86
− 85
....

....

9. What is the abbreviation for **millimetre**? ....

10. 12 − ☐ = 10

My score: ──── / **10**

My time: ....
minutes seconds

www.prim-ed.com Prim-Ed Publishing®

Minute 31

Name: .... **Date:** ....

1. 8 x 2 = ...

2. Ben's party starts at 2.00 pm. His party lasts 2 hours.

   What time does it end? ....

3. 　73
   － 38
   　.........

   　.........

4. There are .... angles and .... sides on the shape.

5. 28 ÷ 4 = ...

6. 　58
   ＋ 26
   　.........

   　.........

7. What is the abbreviation for **hour**? ....

8. $3\overline{)12}$

For Questions 9 and 10, circle the figure that is congruent (same shape and size) to the shaded figure.

9.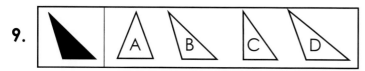

10.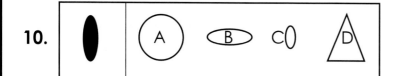

My score: $\dfrac{}{10}$

My time: ....
　　　　　　　　　　minutes　　　　　seconds

Minute 32

Name: .... Date: ....

1. Write the fraction of the shaded area. ....

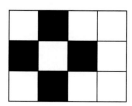

2. This is an angle.

   Circle: True or False

3. 36 ÷ 4 = ...

4. 6 x 6 = ...

5. The perimeter of the shape is 20.

   Circle: True or False

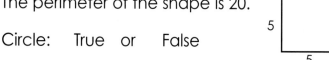

6. 3⟌12

7. The expanded form of 432 is .... + ... + ...

8.   24
    + 38
    ....

    ....

9.   63
    − 28
    ....

    ....

10. Mark bought 18 jelly frogs. He gave 9 of them to his brother. How many jelly frogs did Mark keep for himself?

    .... jelly frogs

My score: ____ / 10   My time: ....
                                    minutes   seconds

Maths minutes

www.prim-ed.com   Prim-Ed Publishing®

Minute 33

Name: .... **Date:** ....

1. 78
   + 15
   ....

   ....

2. Write the next two numbers in the pattern.

   8, 16, 24, 32, 40, ..., ...

3. The area of the shape is 6 square units.

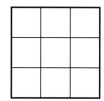

   Circle: True   or   False

4. 30 ÷ 5 = ...

5. 9 x 2 = ...

6. What time does the clock show?   11. ....

7. Circle how many centimetres equal 1 metre.

   10   100   1000

8. 4)‾1‾6‾ □

9. What is the abbreviation for **second**? ....

10. 75
    − 37
    ....

    ....

Minute 34

Name: .... **Date:** ....

1. Sam buys milk in the cafe for 55p.
   He gives the person who served him 70p.

   How much change will he receive? ....

2.   24
   + 48
   ....

   ....

3. The area of the shape is 12 square units.

   Circle: True   or   False

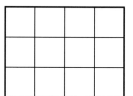

4.   80
   − 48
   ....

   ....

5. 10 x 2 = ...

6. 17 + ... = 28

7. Circle the abbreviation for **centimetre**.   cm   Cm   cM

8. 45 ÷ 5 = ...

   For Questions 9 and 10, round the number to the nearest ten.

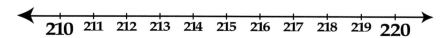

210   211   212   213   214   215   216   217   218   219   220

9. 212 rounds to ....

10. 217 rounds to ....

My score: ___
    10

My time: ....
              minutes   seconds

www.prim-ed.com   Prim-Ed Publishing®

Minute 35

Name: ....   Date: ....

1. Name the 3-D shape. ....

2. 92
   − 54
   ....

   ....

3. The area of the shape is 6 square units.

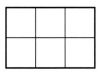

   Circle: True   or   False

4. 6 x 6 = ...

5. 40 ÷ 5 = ...

6. 15 − .... = 5

7. 36
   + 45
   ....

   ....

Use <, > or = to complete Questions 8 to 10.

8. 580 579

9. 999 899

10. 624 524

My score: _____
          10

My time: ....
          minutes   seconds

Minute 36

Name: .... Date: ....

1. 9 x 6 = ...

2. 10 millimetres = 1 centimetre

   80 mm = ... cm

3. 30 ÷ 6 = ...

4. £2.00 – 30p = £ ....

5.   36
    + 55
    ....

    ....

6. Write the missing numbers in the pattern.

   25, ..., 35, ... 45, ..., 55

7.   67
    – 18
    ....

    ....

Use the pie chart to complete Questions 8 to 10.

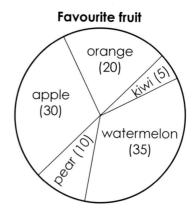

Favourite fruit

8. Which fruit is the most popular?

   ....

9. Which fruit is the least popular?

   ....

10. The number of people who like apples the best is equal to the number of people who like pears and which other fruit?

    ....

My score: ___
10

My time: ....
         minutes   seconds

www.prim-ed.com   Prim-Ed Publishing®

Minute 37

Name: .... Date: ....

1. 9 x 5 = ...

2. 1000 + 300 + 20 + 1 = ...

3.   36
   − 27
   ....

   ....

4. 3)‾15‾ □

5. + = £............ ....

6. Write 21, 12, 201 and 210 in order from **least** to **greatest**. ....

7.   43
   + 55
   ....

   ....

8. Joel races a radio-controlled car. He has 3 sets of 4 batteries. How many batteries does he have altogether?

   .... batteries

In Questions 9 and 10, do the figures have symmetry? Circle yes or no.
If yes, draw the line of symmetry.

9. yes   no

10. yes   no

My score: _____
10

My time: ....
         minutes   seconds

Minute 38

Name: .... **Date:** ....

1. Circle the name of the shape.

   pentagon   hexagon   octagon

2. 1 pound = ... pence

3. What does decade mean? .... years

4. 8 x 8 = ...

5. What is the perimeter of the shape? .... cm

   5 cm

   3 cm □ 3 cm

   5 cm

6. 42 ÷ 6 = ...

7. 21 ÷ 7 = ...

8.   57
   + 42
   ....

   ....

9.   84
   − 49
   ....

   ....

10. Mary plants 4 rows with 5 sunflowers in each row.

    How many sunflowers does she plant in all? .... sunflowers

My score: ‾‾‾‾‾
10

My time: ....
                minutes   seconds

www.prim-ed.com   Prim-Ed Publishing®

Minute 39

Name: .... **Date:** ....

1. $2 \times 9 =$ ....

2. This is an angle. Circle: True   or   False

3. $14 \div 7 =$ ....

4.   348
     + 41
     ‥‥‥‥

     ‥‥‥‥

5. $6 \times$ .... $= 24$

6. Write the times in order trom **earliest** to **latest**.

   6.45 pm   2.15 pm   4.15 pm

   ....

7.   85
     − 49
     ‥‥‥‥

     ‥‥‥‥

8. Write the number **three hundred and fifty-eight**. ....

For Questions 9 and 10, write how much time has passed.

9. 1.15 to 3.45 = 2 hours and .... minutes

10. 2.00 to 4.15 = 2 hours and .... minutes

My score: ____ / **10**   **My time:** ....
                                          minutes   seconds

Minute 40

Name: .... Date: ....

1. 3 x 7 = ...

2. 24 ÷ 8 = ...

3.   82
    − 55
    ....

    ....

4.   475
    + 81
    ....

    ....

5. 2 x .... = 16

6. Measure line $\overrightarrow{AB}$. .... cm   A •———————• B

7. Each helicopter seats 5 people. 15 people need to travel.

   How many helicopters are needed? .... helicopters

Use <, > or = to complete Questions 8 to 10.

8. 120 201

9. 1005 1000

10. 555 584

My score: $\dfrac{}{10}$

My time: ....
                   minutes   seconds

www.prim-ed.com   Prim-Ed Publishing®

Minute 41

Name: .... Date: ....

1. 6 x 8 = ...

2. 40 ÷ 8 = ...

3. 226
   + 37
   ....

   ....

4. There are .... angles and .... sides on this shape.

5. 90
   − 25
   ....

   ....

6. There are 8 nests in the henhouse. In each nest there are 4 eggs.

   How many eggs are there altogether? .... eggs

7. Write the number **four hundred and eighty-six**. ....

8. 7 x .... = 35

For Questions 9 and 10, circle the figure that is congruent (same shape and size) to the shaded figure.

9.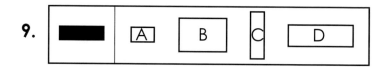

10.

My score: ___
        10

My time: ....
             minutes   seconds

Minute 42

Name: .... **Date:** ....

1. Write the fraction of the shaded area. ....

2. 400 + 20 + 3 = ...

3. 8 x 8 = ...

4. Circle how many metres are in 1 kilometre.

   10   100   1000

5. 72 ÷ 8 = ...

6. 3)‾1‾8‾ (with box above)

7.   262
   + 19
   ....

   ....

8. Which number is the dividend? ....   5̄ over 7)35

Use <, > or = to complete Questions 9 and 10.

9. 126 226

10. 1008 1801

My score: ‾‾‾‾‾ **10**   **My time:** ....
                                          minutes   seconds

Maths minutes   www.prim-ed.com   Prim-Ed Publishing®

Minute 43

Name: .... **Date:** ....

1. 6 x 4 = ...

2. Evan wants to buy 6 pencils. They are 8p each.

   How much money does he need to buy the pencils? ....

3. Write the next two numbers in the pattern.   9, 18, 27, 36, 45, ..., ...

4. 4)‾28‾ with □ on top

5. 56 ÷ 8 = ...

6. What time does the clock show? ....

7.   518
    + 27
    ‾‾‾‾‾

    ‾‾‾‾‾

8.   148
    − 36
    ‾‾‾‾‾

    ‾‾‾‾‾

Use the bar graph to complete Questions 9 and 10.

9. The favourite TV show
   received how many votes?

   .... votes

10. Which two TV shows are watched
    by an equal number of people?

    ....

    and ....

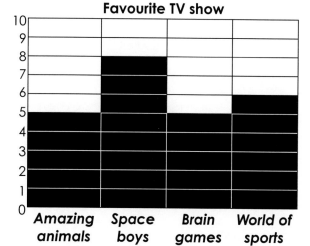

My score: ___
          10

My time: ....
              minutes   seconds

Minute 44

Name: .... **Date:** ....

1. Aram buys a pad of paper for 75p. He gives the shop keeper £1.00.

   How much change will he receive? ....

2. 8 x 3 = ...

3. 845
    + 38
    ....

    ....

4. The volume of the shape is 8 cubic units. Circle: True   or   False

   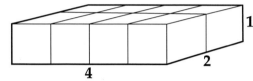

   length x width x height = volume

   4 x 2 x 1 = ... cubic units

5. 28 ÷ 7 = ...

6. Each bus seats 20 people. There are 2 buses.

   How many people can go on the trip? .... people

7. 5)‾30‾

8. 174
    – 43
    ....

    ....

For Questions 9 and 10, round the number to the nearest ten.

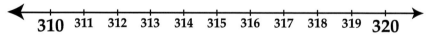

9. 313 rounds to ....

10. 318 rounds to ....

My score: ——— / **10**   **My time:** ....
                                              minutes   seconds

Minute 45

Name: .... **Date:** ....

1. Circle the name of this 3-D shape.

    sphere   cube   cylinder   pyramid

2. 9 x 7 = ...

3. The area of the shape is 4 square centimetres.

    Circle: True   or   False

4. 4)28‾ (with box above)

5. 673
    + 19
    ....

    ....

6. Complete the fact family.

    6 x 8 = ...   48 ÷ 8 = ...

    8 x 6 = 48   48 ÷ 6 = 8

7. There are 7 mother geese. Each mother goose has 4 goslings.

    How many goslings are there in total? .... goslings

8. 243
    − 33
    ....

    ....

9. £1.00 − 60p = ...

10. Measure line $\overrightarrow{AB}$.

    $\overrightarrow{AB}$ = ... cm

My score: _____
10

My time: ....
                    minutes   seconds

Prim-Ed Publishing®   www.prim-ed.com

Minute 46

Name: .... **Date:** ....

1. 9 x 4 = ...

2. Write the number **one thousand, four hundred and thirty-three**.

....

3. Complete the fact family.   7 x 5 = ...   35 ÷ 5 = ...

5 x 7 = 35   35 ÷ 7 = 5

4. The volume of the shape is 18 cubic units. Circle: True   or   False

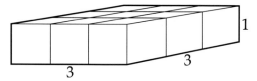

l x w x h = volume

3 x 3 x 1 = ... cubic units

5.   255
     − 48
     ....

     ....

6.   £0.96
     +£0.56
     ....

     ....

7.   542
     + 22
     ....

     ....

8. 7)‾42‾ $\boxed{6}$ Which number is the **divisor**? ....

Use <, > or = to complete Questions 9 to 10.

9. 524 542   **10.**   856 685

My score: $\dfrac{}{10}$ **My time:** ....
                                                        minutes   seconds

www.prim-ed.com   Prim-Ed Publishing®

Minute 47

Name: ....   Date: ....

1. 7 x 8 = ...

2. The expanded form of 3864 is 3000 + ... + ... + 4.

3.   566
  + 55
  ....

  ....

4. The volume of the shape is 18 cubic units.   Circle: True   or   False

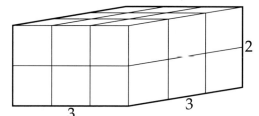

l x w x h = volume

3 x 3 x 2 = ... cubic units

5. Gus has £2.25. He rakes the leaves in the yard and earns another £2.25.

How much money does he have altogether? ....

6. 1000 kilograms = ... tonne

7.   353
  – 205
  ....

  ....

8. 45 ÷ 9 = ...

In Questions 9 and 10, does the figure have symmetry? Write yes or no.
If yes, draw the line of symmetry.

9. .... 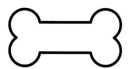   **10.** ....

My score: _____
10

My time: ....
                                  minutes   seconds

Minute 48

Name: .... **Date:** ....

1. Circle the name of the shape.

   pentagon   hexagon   octagon

2. This is a right angle.

   Circle: True   or   False

3. 54 ÷ 9 = ...

4. If apples cost 15p each, how many can be bought for 30p? ....

For Questions 5 and 6, would you choose grams or kilograms to weigh each?
Circle grams or kilograms.

5.   grams   or   kilograms

6.    grams   or   kilograms

7. What is the perimeter of the shape? .... cm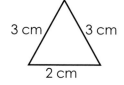

8. Carrie pays 35p for 7 sweets. How much did each sweet cost? ....

9. 414
   + 26
   ....

   ....

10. 326
    – 250
    ....

    ....

Minute 49

Name: .... Date: ....

1. £5.00 – £3.70 = ...

2. 237
   + 33
   ....

   ....

3. 36 ÷ 9 = ...

4. The volume of the shape is 8 cubic centimetres. Circle: True   or   False

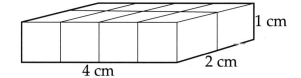

   l x w x h = volume

   4 cm x 2 cm x 1 cm = ... cm^3

5. .... L = 1000 mL

6. $9\overline{)72}$ $\square$

7. 9 x 6 = ...

8. 870
   – 328
   ....

   ....

For Questions 9 and 10, write how much time has passed in hours and minutes.

9. 8.15 to 10.15 = ... hours and .... minutes

10. 7.20 to 9.40 = ... hours and .... minutes

---

My score: $\dfrac{}{10}$ My time: ....
                                              minutes   seconds

Minute 50

Name: .... Date: ....

1. 6 x 7 = ...

For Questions 2 and 3, would you choose kilograms or tonnes to weigh each?
Circle the answer.

2.    kilograms   or   tonnes

3.    kilograms   or   tonnes

4.   215
     – 146
     ....

     ....

5. How long is line $\overrightarrow{AB}$? .... cm   A •———• B

6.   258
     + 168
     ....

     ....

7.   4)‾28‾

8. 56 ÷ 8 = ...

For Questions 9 and 10, write the number.

9. 2000 + 600 + 30 + 9 = ...

10. three hundred and twenty-two ....

My score: ——— 10   My time: ....
                                    minutes   seconds

www.prim-ed.com   Prim-Ed Publishing®

Minute 51

Name: .... Date: ....

1. 5 x 6 = ...

2.   325
      + 115
      ....

      ....

3. 63 ÷ 9 = ...

4. There are .... angles and .... sides on this shape.

For Questions 5 and 6, circle the best answer for each.

5. A rubber raft weighs about:

   15 g   15 kg   5 t.

6. An adult elephant weighs about:

   4 g   4 kg   4 t.

7. There are 7 horses on the farm. Each horse has 4 horseshoes.

   How many horseshoes is that altogether? .... horseshoes

8.   694
      − 589
      ....

      ....

9. 8)‾48‾ ⌐6⌐   Which number is the **divisor**? ....

10. Circle the figure that is congruent to the shaded figure.

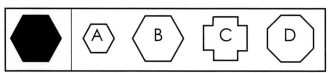

My score: —— / **10**   My time: ....
                                         minutes   seconds

Minute 52

Name: .... **Date:** ....

1. Write the fraction of the shaded area. ....

2. The expanded form of 5455 is

   .... + 400 + ... + 5.

3. 6 x 8 = ...

4. 1 metre = 100 centimetres

   $\frac{1}{2}$ metre = ... centimetres

For Questions 5 and 6, circle the best answer for each.

5. An apple weighs about:

   110 g   11 kg   1 t.

6. A truck weighs about:

   500 g   50 kg   5 t.

7. 0 x 8 = ...

8.   429
   + 330
   ....

   ....

9.   786
   − 579
   ....

   ....

10. Each motorcycle carries 2 people. 12 people need to travel.

    How many motorcycles are needed? .... motorcycles

My score: $\dfrac{}{10}$ **My time:** ....

                                            minutes   seconds

www.prim-ed.com   Prim-Ed Publishing®

Minute 53

Name: .... Date: ....

1. 3 x 9 = ...

2. Ivy wants to buy 8 erasers. They are 5p each.

   How much money does she need to buy the erasers? ....p

3. Write the next two numbers in the pattern.

   7, 14, 21, 28, 35, ..., ...

4. 742
   + 135
   ....

   ....

5. 81 ÷ 9 = ...

6. What time does the clock show?   5............

7. 2)‾19̄ □r ....

Use the pie chart to complete Questions 8 to10.

8. Which dessert is least popular?

   ....

9. Which two desserts are equally popular?

   .... and

   ....

10. Which dessert is most popular?

   ....

Favourite kind of dessert

My score: _____
         10

My time: ....
         minutes   seconds

Minute 54

Name: .... **Date:** ....

1. Susan buys a box of crayons for £1.50.
   She gives the shop assistant £2.00.

   How much change will she receive? ....

2. 8 x 5 = ...

3.   971
     – 583
     ....

     ....

4. The volume of the shape is 12 cubic centimetres.

   Circle: True   or   False

   l x w x h = volume

   3 cm x 2 cm x 2 cm = ... cm^3

   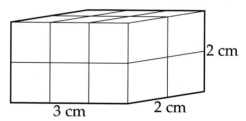

5. 0 x 3 = ...

6.   395
     + 205
     ....

     ....

7. $5\overline{)34}$ □ r ....

8. $6\overline{)36}$ [6]   Which number is the **dividend**? ....

For Questions 9 and 10, round the number to the nearest hundred. Circle the answer.

9. 140 rounds to: 100   200.
10. 180 rounds to: 100   200.

My score: $\dfrac{\quad}{10}$ **My time:** ....
                                             minutes   seconds

www.prim-ed.com   Prim-Ed Publishing®

Minute 55

Name: .... **Date:** ....

1. Name the 3-D shape. ....

2. 9 x 5 = ...

3. What is the area of the shape? .... square centimetres

6 cm

4 cm

length x width = area

4. 306
   + 463
   ....

   ....

5. 28 ÷ 4 = ...

6. 2)‾1‾4‾ □

7. 568
   − 387
   ....

   ....

Use <, > or = to complete Questions 8 to 10.

8.   □

9. □

10. □

My score: ———
            10

My time: ....
           minutes   seconds

Minute 56

Name: .... Date: ....

1. 7 x 7 = ...

2. 8)‾56‾ □

3. 0 x 5 = ...

4. There are .... faces on this 3-D shape.

5. 7940 = ... + ... + 40

6.   330
  + 127
  ....

  ....

7.   824
  − 378
  ....

  ....

For Questions 8 to 10, write the number.

8. two thousand, three hundred and forty-one ....

9. 300 + 50 + 9 ....

10. five hundred and ninety-six ....

My score: ___
10

My time: ....
      minutes   seconds

Minute 57

Name: ....   Date: ....

1. 9 x 8 = ...

2. The expanded form of 8311 is .... + ... + ... + ...

3. 2)$\overline{50}$ $\square$

4. 3 decades = ... years

5. Hannah has £3.25. Her sister, Camille, has £4.75.

   How much money do they have altogether? £............

6.   724
   − 396
   ....

   ....

7. 63 ÷ 7 = ...

8.   135
   + 173
   ....

   ....

In Questions 9 and 10, does the figure have symmetry? Write yes or no.

If yes, draw the line of symmetry.

9. ....

10. ....

My score: $\dfrac{}{10}$ My time: ....
                                                minutes   seconds

Minute 58

Name: .... Date: ....

1. Circle the name of the shape.

    pentagon   hexagon   octagon

2. This is a right angle. Circle: True   or   False

3. 7 x 5 = ...

4. Dominic pays 30p for 6 pencils. How much did each pencil cost? ....p

5. What is the perimeter of the shape? ....

6. 42 ÷ 6 = ...

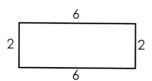

7. There are 14 marbles divided into groups of 3.

    There are .... groups of 3

    with .... remaining marbles.

8. 205
    + 341
    ....

    ....

9. 921
    – 287
    ....

    ....

10. The farmer ploughs 8 rows. He plants 7 seedlings in each row.

    How many seedlings does he plant in all? .... seedlings

My score: ___
10

My time: ....
                minutes   seconds

Maths minutes

Minute 59

Name: .... **Date:** ....

1. 6 x 8 = ...

2. £5.00 – £1.40 = ...

3.
```
   35
   52
 + 11
 ........
```

   ....

4. 28 ÷ 7 = ...

5. 1 week = ... days

6.
```
   532
 – 186
 ..........
```

   ....

7. 0 x 9 = ...

8. 6)‾2‾9‾ □ r ....

For Questions 9 and 10, write what time it will be.

9. In 1 hour it will be

   ....

10. In $1\frac{1}{2}$ hours it will be

   ....

My score: $\dfrac{}{10}$

My time: ....
   minutes   seconds

Minute 60

Name: .... Date: ....

1. 4 x 9 = ...

2. How long is line $\overrightarrow{AB}$? .... cm   A ———————— B

3. 24
    48
+ 34
  ....

  ....

For Questions 4 and 5, write the numbers.

4. four thousand, one hundred and sixty-two ....

5. seven hundred and three ....

6. 821
 – 497
  ....

  ....

7. Jason is working at a pet shop. There are 54 mice. He divides them evenly into 9 cages.

How many mice are in each cage? .... mice

Use <, > or = to complete Questions 8 to 10.

8. 1638 ☐ 738

9. 845 ☐ 548

10. 112 ☐ 211

My score: ——— 10

My time: ....
                      minutes   seconds

www.prim-ed.com   Prim-Ed Publishing®

Minute 61

Name: ....   **Date:** ....

1. 865
    − 375
    ....

    ....

2. 32 ÷ 8 = ...

3.   73
      32
   + 21
   ....

   ....

4. There are .... angles and .... sides on the shape.

5. $5\overline{)21}$ □ r ....

6.   23
   × 2
   ....

   ....

Use <, > or = to complete Questions 7 and 8.

7. 4206 ☐ 5206   **8.** 3929 ☐ 3729

For Questions 9 and 10, circle the figure that is congruent to the shaded figure.

9.   A   B   C   D

10.   A   B   C   D

My score: $\dfrac{\quad}{10}$ **My time:** ....
                                               minutes   seconds

Minute 62

Name: .... **Date:** ....

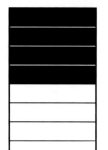

1. Write the fraction of the shaded area. ....

2. The expanded form of 3024 is .... + 20 + ...

3.   32
       x 2
       ....

       ....

4. 1000 grams = 1 kilogram

   5000 grams = ... kilograms

5. 4) 36

6. Write the missing numbers in the pattern.

   6, 12, ..., ..., 30, 36

7.   38
       32
     + 21
       ....

       ....

Use <, > or = to complete Questions 8 to 10.

8. 5340 ☐ 5940

9. 435 ☐ 316

10. 652 ☐ 228

My score: ── 10

My time: ....
                   minutes   seconds

www.prim-ed.com   Prim-Ed Publishing®

Minute 63

Name: .... **Date:** ....

1. 39
    42
    + 71
    ....

    ....

2. Write the missing numbers in the pattern.   4, 8, ..., 16, 20, 24, ..., 32

3. Isaac wants to buy 7 books at a garage sale. They are 10p each.

    How much money does he need to buy the books? ....

4. 35 ÷ 7 = ...

5. 14
    x 2
    ....

    ....

6. What time does the clock show? ....

7. 8)‾3‾2‾ (with box above)

Use the bar graph to complete Questions 8 to 10.

8. How many people voted for a favourite wild animal?

    .... people

9. How many more people chose the tiger than the deer as a favourite animal?

    .... more people

10. Which two animals were equally popular?

    ....

Favourite wild animal

(Bar graph with y-axis 0–10: Tiger = 7, Elephant = 3, Deer = 2, Bear = 3)

My score: ____
10

My time: ....
minutes   seconds

Name: .... **Date:** ....

1. Chris buys a hamburger for £3.50. He pays with a £5.00 note.

   How much change will he receive? ....

2.   742
     − 406
     ....

   ....

3.   32
       7
    + 11
     ....

   ....

4. What is the volume of this shape?

   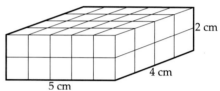

   5 cm x 4 cm x 2 cm = ... cubic centimetres

5. $5\overline{)39}$ □ r ....

6. 64 ÷ 8 = ...

7.   33
     x 3
     ....

   ....

For Questions 8 to 10, round the number to the nearest hundred. Circle the answer.

8. 250 rounds to: 200   300.

9. 536 rounds to: 500   600.

10. 263 rounds to: 200   300.

My score: $\dfrac{}{10}$ **My time:** ....
                                                 minutes   seconds

Minute 65

Name: .... **Date:** ....

1. Circle the name of the 3-D shape.

    sphere   cone   cylinder   pyramid

2. $4\overline{)28}$ with $\square$ above

3. What is the area of this shape? .... square centimetres

    6 cm

 2 cm [rectangle]   length x width = area

For Questions 4 and 5, write the number.

4. 4000 + 300 + 6 = ...

5. 9000 + 500 + 20 + 2 = ...

For Questions 6 and 7, circle the best answer for each.

> A 5 pound note weighs about 1 gram.
>
> A thick book weighs about 1 kilogram.

6. A bicycle weighs about: 12 g   120 g   12 kg.

7. A 10 pence coin weighs about: 3 g   300 g   3 kg.

8. How long is line $\overrightarrow{AB}$? .... cm A ————— B

9. Circle the correct answer. $\frac{6}{10}$ = 0.6 or 0.06 ?

10. What type of triangle is this? ....

    scalene   isosceles   equilateral

My score: $\dfrac{}{10}$ **My time:** ....
                                       minutes   seconds

Prim-Ed Publishing®   www.prim-ed.com

Minute 66

Name: .... **Date:** ....

1. Eden wants to buy 5 rabbits. Each rabbit costs £10.00.

   How much money does Eden need to buy the rabbits? £............

2. 28 ÷ 7 = ...

3. Write the missing numbers in the pattern.   38, 36, ..., 32, ..., 28, 26

4. This 3-D shape has how many faces? ....

5. $\dfrac{\boxed{}}{5)\overline{42}}$ r ....

6.   11
   x 6
   ....

   ....

7.   926
   − 285
   ....

   ....

Use <, > or = to complete Questions 8 to 10.

8.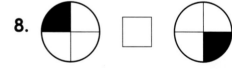

9.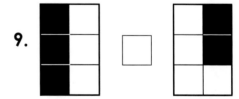

10.

My score: ——— **10**   **My time:** ....
                                          minutes   seconds

Minute 67

Name: .... **Date:** ....

1. How many centimetres make up $5\frac{1}{2}$ metres? Circle the answer.

   55 cm   505 cm   550 cm

2. The expanded form of 4707 is .... + 700 + 7.

3. 18 ÷ 3 = ...

4. Write the missing number in the pattern.

   99, ..., 79, ..., 59, 49

5. What time does the clock show? ....

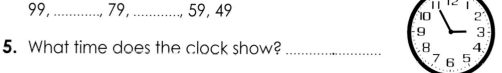

6. Miles wants to buy a bat for £2.00, a ball for 50p and a glove for £3.00. How much money does he need to buy all three items?

   £........................

7.   23
      x 3
     ....

     ....

8.   723
    − 402
    ....

    ....

For Questions 9 and 10, write the number.

9. six hundred and seventy-nine ....

10. nine hundred ....

My score: $\frac{\quad\quad}{10}$

My time: ....
                   minutes   seconds

Minute 68

Name: ....   **Date:** ....

1.   36
     11
   + 43
   ....

   ....

2. This is a right angle.

   Circle: True   or   False

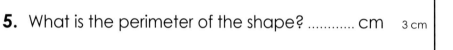

3. 24 ÷ 4 = ...

4. Bailey pays 45p for 9 plastic spiders.

   How much did each spider cost? ....p

5. What is the perimeter of the shape? .... cm

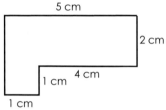

6.   65
    x 1
    ....

    ....

7. Write the missing numbers in the pattern.   2, 4, 8, ..., 32, ...

8.   806
   − 457
   ....

   ....

Use the pie chart to complete Questions 9 and 10.

9. Which insect is the most popular? ....

10. Is the bee more or less popular than the

    butterfly? ....

Favourite insect

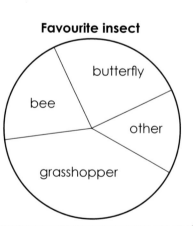

My score: ___
            10

My time: ....
                      minutes   seconds

www.prim-ed.com   Prim-Ed Publishing®

Minute 69

Name: .... Date: ....

1. Name the shape. ....

2. 1 t = 1000 kg $4\frac{1}{2}$ t = ... kg

3.   22
     x 2
     ....

     ....

4.   425
     – 16
     ....

     ....

For Questions 5 and 6, circle the fraction of the shaded area.

5. $\frac{1}{2}$ $\frac{1}{3}$ $\frac{5}{8}$ $\frac{3}{4}$

6. $\frac{1}{2}$ $\frac{2}{3}$ $\frac{1}{4}$ $\frac{3}{4}$

7. 21 ÷ 7 = ...

8. 3000 + 300 + 10 + 4 = ...

For Questions 9 and 10, write what time it was.

9. 1 hour before

   ....

10. I hour and 15 minutes

    before ....

My score: $\frac{\quad\quad}{10}$ My time: ....

.... minutes   .... seconds

Name: .... **Date:** ....

1. 45 ÷ 5 = ...

2. James has a book that has 64 pages. If he reads 8 pages each day, how many days will it take him to finish the book? .... days

3. 12 + 19 + 17 = ...

4. Measure line $\overrightarrow{AB}$. .... cm   A •——————• B

For Questions 5 and 6, circle the fraction that tells which part is shaded.

5. $\frac{1}{2}$ $\frac{1}{3}$ $\frac{2}{3}$ $\frac{3}{4}$

6. $\frac{1}{2}$ $\frac{2}{3}$ $\frac{1}{4}$ $\frac{3}{4}$

7.   30
    x 5
    ....

    ....

Use the line graph to complete Questions 8 to 10.

8. What was the temperature on Sunday?

   ....

9. Which day recorded the highest

   temperature? ....

10. How many degrees higher was Saturday's temperature than Sunday's?

    .... degrees Celsius

Highest temperature by day

(Degrees Celsius)

My score: ——
          10

My time: ....
                    minutes   seconds

Minute 71

Name: .... Date: ....

1. 246
   + 129
   ....

   ....

2. There are .... angles and .... sides on the shape.

For Questions 3 and 4, write the fraction of the shaded area.

3.   ....

4.   ....

5. 6)‾48‾ □

6. Write the missing numbers in the pattern. 100, 110, ..., 130, ..., 150, 160

Use <, > or = to complete Questions 7 and 8.

7. 711 ☐ 171

8. 102 ☐ 201

For Questions 9 and 10, circle the figure that is congruent (same shape and size) to the shaded figure.

9.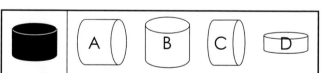

10.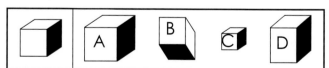

My score: ──
          10

My time: ....
                    minutes   seconds

Name: .... **Date:** ....

1. Write the fraction of the shaded area. ....

2. The expanded form of 4120 is .... + 100 + ...

3.   500
  + 806
  ....

  ....

4. 1 kilometre = 1000 metres

  5 kilometres = ... metres

5. 42 ÷ 7 = ...

6.   24
  x 2
  ....

  ....

7. In 84 + 11 = 95, the number 95 is called the **sum**.

  Circle: True   or   False

Use <, > or = to complete Questions 8 to 10.

8. 989 ☐ 998

9. 419 ☐ 941

10. 491 ☐ 419

My score: $\dfrac{}{10}$ **My time:** ....
                                                  minutes   seconds

Minute 73

Name: .... **Date:** ....

1. 32
    x 4
    ....

    ....

2. Write the missing numbers in the pattern. 6, 12, ..., 24, ..., 36, 42

3. Britney wants to buy 7 sweets. They are 5p each.

    How much money does she need to buy the sweets? ....

4. 56 ÷ 7 = ...

5. 924
    + 209
    ....

    ....

6. What time does the clock show? ....

7. Write the numbers 149, 185, 158 and 194 from **least** to **greatest**.

    ....

Use the pie chart to complete Questions 8 to 10.

8. Turtles are more popular than

    which other animal? ....

9. If 15 people picked dogs, then approximately

    how many people picked cats? .... people

10. Did more people prefer fish or

    turtles? ....

Favourite pet

My score: ——
10

My time: ....
             minutes   seconds

Minute 74

Name: .... **Date:** ....

For Questions 1 and 2, write the number.

1. eight hundred and twenty-one ....

2. five thousand, two hundred and forty-two ....

3. 36 ÷ 6 = ...

4. What is the volume of the shape? .... cubes

   6 x 2 x 2 = volume

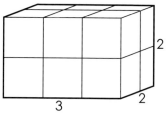

For Questions 5 to 7, circle the place value of the bold digit.

5. 5**7**9   thousands   hundreds   tens   ones

6. 1**9**62   thousands   hundreds   tens   ones

7. **4**270   thousands   hundreds   tens   ones

For Questions 8 to 10, round the number to the nearest hundred. Circle the answer.

8. 521 rounds to: 500   600.

9. 582 rounds to: 500   600.

10. 146 rounds to: 100   200.

My score: ___
10

My time: ....
                minutes   seconds

www.prim-ed.com   Prim-Ed Publishing®

Minute 75

Name: .... **Date:** ....

1. Name the shape. .... ⬭

2. 1250
   + 718
   ....

   ....

6
12

3. What is the area of the shape? .... cubic units

For Questions 4 and 5, write the fraction of the shaded area as a part of the total area.

4.   ....

5.   ....

6. Zoe buys a kite for £3.50. She gives the shop assistant £5.00.

   How much change will she receive? ....

7. 4)̄36

Use <, > or = to complete Questions 8 to 10.

8. 308 ☐ 380

9. 452 ☐ 542

10. 621 ☐ 612

My score: ____ / **10**

My time: ....
                        minutes   seconds

Minute 76

Name: .... Date: ....

1. The film starts at 1.00 pm. It ends at 3.10 pm.

   The film is .... hour(s) and .... minutes long.

2.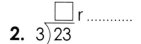
   $\frac{\square}{3)\overline{23}}$ r ....

3.   50
    x 3
   ....

   ....

4. There are .... faces on the 3-D shape.

For Questions 5 to 7, circle the place value of the bold digit.

5. **7**249   thousands   hundreds   tens   ones

6. 43**7**   thousands   hundreds   tens   ones

7. 2**1**70   thousands   hundreds   tens   ones

Use <, > or = to complete Questions 8 to 10.

8.

9.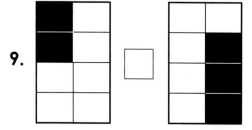

10.

My score: $\dfrac{\quad}{10}$ My time: ....

minutes   seconds

www.prim-ed.com   Prim-Ed Publishing®

Minute 77

Name: .... Date: ....

1. John started playing football at 2.15 pm. His game ended at 3.45 pm.

    His game lasted .... hour(s) and .... minutes.

2. The expanded form of 5148 is 5000 + ... + ... + ...

3.   22
       x 4
       ....

       ....

4. 42 ÷ 6 = ...

5. Aaron earned £1.50 washing a car. He earned £2.50 washing clothes.

    How much money did he earn altogether? ....

**In Questions 6 to 8, how does each 3-D shape look from the top?
Circle the answer.**

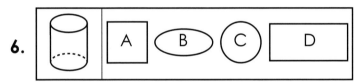

6. A   B   C   D

7. A   B   C   D

8. A   B   C   D

**In Questions 9 and 10, does the figure have a line of symmetry? Write yes
or no. If yes, draw the line of symmetry.**

9.   ....   10.   ....

My score: _____ **10**

My time: ....
                                    minutes   seconds

Name: .... Date: ....

1. 3383
    + 5004
    ....

    ....

2. This is a right angle.

    Circle: True   or   False

3. 53
    x 3
    ....

    ....

4. Clare pays 60p for 12 dice. How much did each die cost? ....p

5. What is the perimeter of the shape? .... units

6. Write the next two numbers in the pattern.

    15, 13, 11, ..., ...

7. 3000 + 400 + 80 + 2 = ...

Use the bar graph to complete Questions 8 to 10.

8. Which type of party was most

    popular? ....

9. How many people preferred a

    pool party? .... people

10. How many more people preferred
    a pizza party to a cinema party?

    .... more people

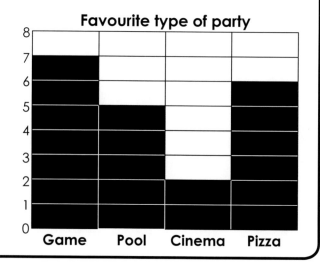

My score: ____
         10

My time: ....
                minutes   seconds

www.prim-ed.com   Prim-Ed Publishing®

Minute 79

Name: ....   **Date:** ....

1. Name the shape. ....

2. $5\overline{)25}$

3. Hannah sold 5 cups of lemonade. Each cup cost 20p.

   How much money did Hannah make? ....

4. 1 m = 100 cm

   $5\frac{1}{2}$ m = ... cm

In questions 5–7, how does the 3-D shape look from the side? Circle the answer.

5.

6.

7.

8. Write the missing numbers in the pattern.

   225, ..., 235, 240, ..., 250, 255

9.   4024
    + 1235
     ....

     ....

10. 3000 + 900 + 40 + 8 = ...

My score: $\frac{\quad\quad}{10}$ **My time:** ....
                                                  minutes   seconds

Minute 80

Name: .... Date: ....

1. Write the number four hundred and twenty-two. ....

2. $18 \div 6 =$ ....

3. How long is line AB? .... cm

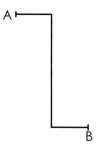

4.   60
      x 4
      ....

      ....

For Questions 5 to 7, circle the place value of the bold digit.

5. **6**499   thousands   hundreds   tens   ones

6. **9**123   thousands   hundreds   tens   ones

7. 4**9**82   thousands   hundreds   tens   ones

Use the pie chart to complete Questions 8 to 10. Circle True or False.

8. The least popular dinosaur is Allosaurus.

   True   False

9. Apatosaurus and Tyrannosaurus are equally popular.

   True   False

10. Raptors are the most popular.

   True   False

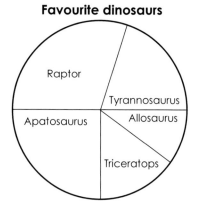

Favourite dinosaurs

My score: $\dfrac{\quad}{10}$ My time: .... minutes   seconds

Minute 81

Name: .... **Date:** ....

1. There are .... angles and .... sides on the shape.

2. 72 ÷ 8 = ...

3. 31
   x 6
   ....

   ....

Use the camp timetable to complete Questions 4 to 6.

4. If Arts/Crafts lasts for 1 hour, at

   what time will it be finished? ....

5. If a camper swam for 2 hours,

   could the camper go on the hike? ....

6. Dinner is 2 hours before the campfire.

   What time is dinner? ....

Camp timetable	
Arts/Crafts 10.15 am	Swimming 1.00 pm
Hike 2.30 pm	Campfire 7.45 pm

Use <, > or = to complete Questions 7 and 8.

7. 947 ☐ 479

8. 652 ☐ 651

For Questions 9 and 10, circle the figure that is congruent to the shaded figure.

9.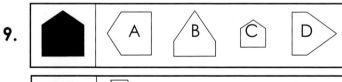

10.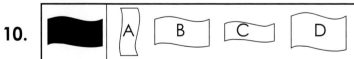

My score: $\dfrac{}{10}$

My time: ....
minutes   seconds

Minute 82

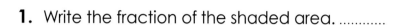

Name: .... **Date:** ....

1. Write the fraction of the shaded area. ....

2. The expanded form of 4890 is .... + ... + 90.

3.   42
       x 3
       ....

       ....

4. 1 kilogram = 1000 grams

   2 kilograms = ... grams

5. 28 ÷ 7 = ...

For Questions 6 and 7, circle the best estimate.

> A five pound note weighs about 1 gram.
>
> A thick book weighs about 1 kilogram.

6. A mouse weighs about: 800 g   8 kg   80 kg.

7. A pair of shoes weighs about: 1 kg   10 kg   100 kg.

Use <, > or = to complete Questions 8 to 10.

8. 485 ☐ 854

9. 325 ☐ 523

10. 412 ☐ 421

My score: ___
10

My time: ....
                                       minutes   seconds

Minute 83

Name: .... Date: ....

1. 32 ÷ 8 = ...

2. Write the missing numbers in the pattern.

    45, 54, ..., 72, ..., 90, 99

3. Ed wants to buy 8 pieces of chewing gum. They are 10p each.

    How much money does he need to buy the chewing gum? ....p

4.   43
     x 3
     ....

     ....

5.   3252
     + 4008
     ....

     ....

6. What time does the clock show? ....

7. The expanded form of 2578 is .... + ... + ... + ...

Use the bar graph to complete Questions 8 to 10.

8. How many letters did Room 12 write? .... letters

9. How many more letters did Room 10 write than Room 14? .... more letters

10. Which room wrote the least amount of letters? ....

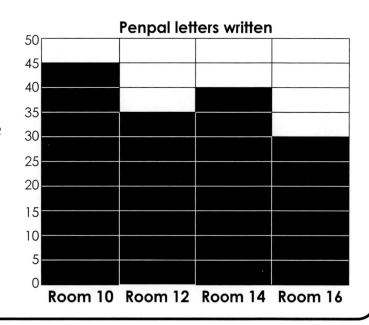

Penpal letters written

My score: _____ / 10   My time: .... minutes .... seconds

Minute 84

Name: .... **Date:** ....

1. Jared buys 2 cinema tickets for £5.10 each.

   How much does he spend? ....

2. What is the volume of this shape? .... cm³

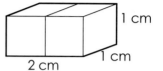

3. 49 ÷ 7 = ...

4.   62

      x 4

      ....

      ....

For Questions 5 to 7, circle the best estimate.

> *A 5 pound note weighs about 1 gram.*
>
> *A thick book weighs about 1 kilogram.*

5. A 20p coin weighs about: 5 g   50 g   5 kg.

6. A car weighs about: 130 g   130 kg   1300 kg.

7. A feather weighs about: 1 g   10 g   100 g.

For Questions 8 to 10, round the number to the place value of the bold digit. Circle the answer.

8. **5**34 rounds to: 500   530   540   600.

9. 2**9**1 rounds to: 200   280   290   300.

10. **8**23 rounds to: 800   820   830   900.

My score: ——— / **10**

My time: ....

                                                      minutes   seconds

Minute 85

Name: .... Date: ....

1. Name the 3-D shape. ....

2. $4\overline{)35}$ $\square$ r ....

3. What is the area of the shape? ....

For Questions 4 to 6, write the number.

4. 3000 + 100 + 40 + 8 = ...

5. 7000 + 60 + 3 = ...

6. 2000 + 900 + 90 + 9 = ...

7. $\begin{array}{r} 51 \\ \times 5 \\ \hline \end{array}$

   ....

8. What will the time be in 2 hours? ....

9. How long is line $\overrightarrow{AB}$? .... cm

10. £4.00 + £1.25 = £...........

Minute 86

Name: .... Date: ....

1. 9040
    + 2831
    ....

    ....

2. 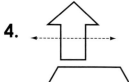 2)‾16‾

3. Name the 3-D shape. ....

In Questions 4 to 6, is the dashed line a line of symmetry? Circle Yes or No.

4. 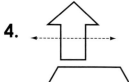   Yes   No

5.    Yes   No

6. 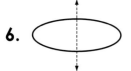   Yes   No

7. Daniel has a rectangular room. He displays two posters on each wall. How many posters does he have displayed in his room?

    .... posters

Use the pie chart to complete Questions 8 to 10.

Favourite items to collect

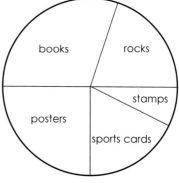

8. Which is the most popular item to collect?

    ....

9. Which is the least popular item to collect?

    ....

10. The number of children who collect sports cards and stamps is

    equal to the number of children who collect ....

My score: ———
              10

My time: ....

....
minutes   seconds

www.prim-ed.com   Prim-Ed Publishing®

Minute 87

Name: .... Date: ....

1. 83
    x 3
    ....

    ....

2. The expanded form of 2322 is .... + ... + ... + ...

3. Write the number **two hundred and sixty-three**. ....

4. 4)‾36‾ □

5. 81 ÷ 9 = ...

6.   4285
    + 3080
    ....

    ....

7.   600
    − 374
    ....

    ....

Use <, > or = to complete Questions 8 to 10.

8. 231 ☐ 321

9. 852 ☐ 825

10. 945 ☐ 954

My score: ‾‾‾‾‾ / 10   **My time:** ....
    minutes   seconds

Minute 88

Name: .... Date: ....

1. 15
    x 5
    ‥‥‥‥

    ‥‥‥‥

2. 7266
    − 3014
    ....

    ....

3. Trudy pays 35p for 7 erasers. How much did each eraser cost? ....

4. 5475
    + 3014
    ....

    ....

5. What is the perimeter of the shape? ....

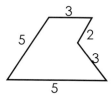

6. 8)⎺7̄2̄

7. How many millilitres in a litre? Circle the answer. 10   100   1000

Use the bar graph to complete Questions 8 to 10.

8. How many cans does each shaded box represent? .... cans

9. How many cans did Room 12 collect? .... cans

10. How many more cans did Room 14 collect than Room 16? .... more cans

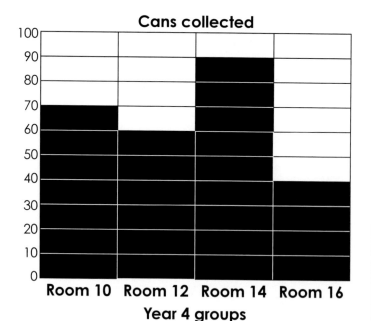

My score: —— 10   My time: ....
                              minutes   seconds

www.prim-ed.com   Prim-Ed Publishing®

Name: .... **Date:** ....

1. Name the 3-D shape. ....

2.   23
    x 3
    ....

    ....

3.   8156
  + 852
  ....

  ....

4. £1.00 – 55p = ...p

5. Ellen reads 15 pages in 1 hour. Last night she read for 2 hours.

    How many pages did she read altogether? .... pages

6. 5)‾45‾ with box above

7. 48 ÷ 8 = ...

8.   9214
  – 7007
  ....

  ....

For Questions 9 and 10, write how much time has passed.

9. 5.15 pm to 7.30 pm = ... hours .... minutes

10. 9.20 pm to 11.40 pm = ... hours .... minutes

My score: _____ **10**

My time: ....
                    minutes   seconds

Name: .... **Date:** ....

1.   32
    x 4
    ....

    ....

2. Nathan helped to sell books at a garage sale. He sold the same number of books each hour. If he sold 27 books in 3 hours, how many books did Nathan sell each hour? .... books

3.   4256
    + 1312
    ....

    ....

4. 45 ÷ 9 = ...

5. 8⟌62 [ ]r ....

6. Write the number **five thousand, two hundred and sixty-five**. ....

7.   7725
    – 2524
    ....

    ....

Use the pie chart to complete questions 8 to 10.

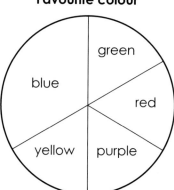

Favourite colour

8. Which colour is most popular? ....

9. Is there a least popular colour? ....

10. If 6 people chose purple, how many people chose yellow? .... people

My score: ___ / 10

My time: ....
            minutes   seconds

Minute 91

Name: .... Date: ....

1. 17
    x 2
    ....

    ....

2. $\boxed{}$r ....
    9$\overline{)57}$

3. There are 54 children at the school fair. If they are evenly

    placed in 6 different games, how many children will be

    playing each game? .... children

4. There are .... angles and .... sides on the shape.

For Questions 5 and 6, write the number.

5. three thousand and twenty-nine ....

6. 4000 + 300 + 60 + 1 = ...

7. 36 ÷ 6 = ...

8. Write the fraction **two-thirds**. ....

For Questions 9 and 10, circle the figure that is congruent (same shape and size) to the shaded figure.

9.

10.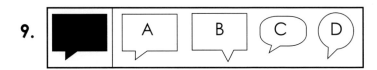

My score: _____
10

My time: ....
              minutes   seconds

Prim-Ed Publishing®   www.prim-ed.com

Minute 92

Name: .... **Date:** ....

1. Write the fraction of the shaded area. ....

2. The expanded form of 5326 is

   .... + ... + ... + ...

3.   45
       x 3
       ....

       ....

4. 4 metres = ... centimetres

In Questions 5 to 7, are the figures congruent? Circle Yes or No.

5.    Yes   No

6.    Yes   No

7.    Yes   No

Use <, > or = to complete Questions 8 to 10.

8. 711 ☐ 171

9. 1547 ☐ 7154

10. 8546 ☐ 8546

My score: $\dfrac{}{10}$ **My time:** ....
                                                            minutes   seconds

Minute 93

Name: .... Date: ....

1. 5834
  – 1212
  ....

  ....

2. Write the missing numbers in the pattern. 80, ..., 70, 65, ..., 55, 50, ...

3. Ava wants to buy 7 crickets. They are 10p each.

  How much money does she need to buy the crickets? ....p

4. 22
  x 6
  ....

  ....

5. 6)‾42‾ (with □ above)

6. What time does the clock show? ....

7. 42 ÷ 7 = ...

Use the line graph to complete Questions 8 to 10.

8. How much time was spent doing

  chores on Sunday? ....

9. Did the chore time increase or
  decrease from Wednesday

  to Thursday? ....

10. Between which two days was the
  greatest increase in time spent doing
  chores? Circle the answer.

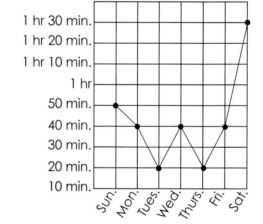

Time spent doing chores

  Tuesday and Wednesday   Thursday and Friday   Friday and Saturday

My score: _____ / 10   My time: .... minutes   .... seconds

Minute 94

Name: .... **Date:** ....

1. Emma buys two chocolate milkshakes for £2.00 each.

   She has £6.00 in her purse. How much will she have left?

   £................

2. Write the fraction **three-eighths**. ....

3. What is the volume of this shape? .... m³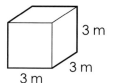

   length x width x height = volume

4.   48
       x 2
      ....

      ....

5. 63 ÷ 7 = ...

For Questions 6 and 7, write the number.

6. 1000 + 400 + 90 + 2 = ...

7. 3000 + 600 + 3 = ...

For Questions 8 to 10, round the place value of the number to the bold digit. Circle the answer.

8. **45**3 rounds to: 400   450   460   500.

9. **39**1 rounds to: 300   380   390   400.

10. **2**93 rounds to: 200   280   290   300.

My score: $\dfrac{}{10}$ **My time:** ....
                                                               minutes   seconds

www.prim-ed.com   Prim-Ed Publishing®

Minute 95

Name: .... Date: ....

1. Circle the name of the 3-D shape.

   cylinder   cone   pyramid   sphere

2. $8\overline{)40}^{\Box}$

3. What is the area of the shape? .... m²

   4 m | 8 m

4. $72 \div 9 = $ ....

5. Lee wants a new computer game. It costs £4.50.
   He gives the shop assistant £10.00. How much change will he receive?

   £....................

6.   51
    x 5
    ....

    ....

7. Write the fraction **five-sixths**. ....

Use the bar graph to complete Questions 8 to 10.

8. Which two pupils ran the furthest? ....

9. Which pupil ran
   seven laps?

   ....

10. Three pupils ran only the
    minimum number of laps.
    What was the minimum
    number of laps?

    .... laps

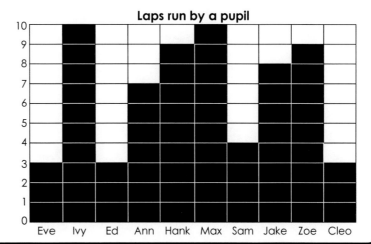

Laps run by a pupil

Eve Ivy Ed Ann Hank Max Sam Jake Zoe Cleo

My score: ____
10

My time: ....
                    minutes   seconds

Name: .... Date: ....

1. Anna had 16 biscuits. She ate half of the biscuits.

   How many biscuits does she have left? .... biscuits

2. $\begin{array}{r} 36 \\ \times 2 \\ \hline \\ \hline \end{array}$

3. 30 ÷ 5 = ...

4. There are .... faces on the 3-D shape.

5. There are .... vertices on the 3-D shape.

6. There are .... edges on the 3-D shape.

7. Write the fraction **three-eighths**. ....

Use <, > or = to complete Questions 8 to 10.

8. ☐

   $\dfrac{1}{4}$ $\dfrac{3}{8}$

9. 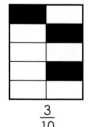 ☐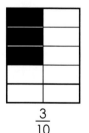

   $\dfrac{3}{10}$ $\dfrac{3}{10}$

10. ☐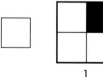

    $\dfrac{2}{8}$ $\dfrac{1}{4}$

My score: $\dfrac{}{10}$

My time: ....
                minutes   seconds

Minute 97

Name: ....   **Date:** ....

1. Evan bought a pair of football boots for £50.00 and a

   mouth guard for £6.95. How much did he spend altogether? £..................

2. The expanded form of 4821 is .... + ... + ... + ...

3.
```
   9935
 - 4765
 ..........

 ..........
```

4.
```
   31
  x 3
 .......

 .......
```

5. 28 ÷ 7 = ...

6.
```
     □ r ............
 6)53
```

7.
```
   4532
 + 7651
 ..........

 ..........
```

Use <, > or = to complete Questions 8 to 10.

8. 524 ☐ 254

9. 5879 ☐ 8756

10. 2741 ☐ 1742

My score: $\dfrac{}{10}$

My time: ....
                    minutes   seconds

Minute 98

Name: .... Date: ....

1. 4125
   + 580
   ....

   ....

2. 8)‾5‾6‾ $\Box$

3. Patricia paid 90p for 9 rubber balls. How much did each ball cost? ....p

4. 32
   x 3
   ....

   ....

5. What is the perimeter of the shape? .... cm

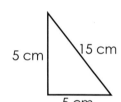
5 cm   15 cm
   5 cm

6. 56 ÷ 8 = ...

7. Write the fraction **four-tenths**. ....

Use the pictogram to complete Questions 8 to 10.

Pupils' birthdays

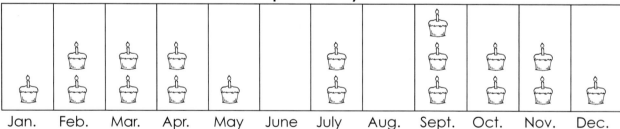

| Jan. | Feb. | Mar. | Apr. | May | June | July | Aug. | Sept. | Oct. | Nov. | Dec. |

(Each 🧁 equals two pupils.)

8. Which month has the most birthdays? ....

9. How many pupils have a birthday in August? .... pupils

10. Which three months have only two pupils with birthdays?

   ....

My score: ――――
        10

My time: ....
                minutes   seconds

Minute 99

Name: .... Date: ....

1. The netball court has 4 rows of seats. 22 people can sit in each row.

   How many people can watch netball? .... people

2. 56 ÷ 7 = ...

3. 1 centimetre = 10 millimetres

   $8\frac{1}{2}$ cm = ... mm

4.   34
     x 2
     ....

     ....

5. £2.20 + £1.80 = £............

For Questions 6 to 8, write the fraction.

6. six-tenths ....

7. one-half ....

8. two-fifths ....

For Questions 9 and 10, write how much time has passed.

9. 5.15 pm to 10.30 pm = ... hours and .... minutes

10. 7.30 pm to 9.40 pm = ... hours and .... minutes

My score: ____ / 10

My time: ....
         minutes   seconds

Minute 100

Name: .... **Date:** ....

1. $\begin{array}{r} 1589 \\ + \ 607 \\ \hline \end{array}$ ....

2. $\begin{array}{r} 7432 \\ - \ 4282 \\ \hline \end{array}$ ....

3. 54 ÷ 6 = ...

4. $\begin{array}{r} 21 \\ \times \ 4 \\ \hline \end{array}$ ....

    ....

5. $\overset{\boxed{}\ r \ ....}{5\overline{)\ 49}}$

Use <, > or = to complete Questions 6 and 7.

6. 788 $\boxed{}$ 877

7. 5465 $\boxed{}$ 5645

Use the line graph to complete Questions 8 to 10.

8. Which month received the most
    rain? ....

9. How many centimetres of rain fell
    in October? .... cm

10. Which months received 4 centimetres
    of rain?
    .... and ....

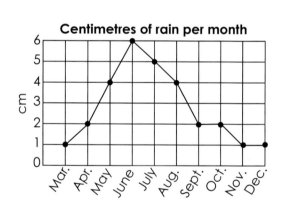

Centimetres of rain per month

My score: $\dfrac{}{10}$

My time: ....
minutes   seconds

www.prim-ed.com   Prim-Ed Publishing®

Minute answer key

Minute 1
1. 10
2. 3
3. odd
4. 6
5. 8
6. 5
7. 3
8. football
9. false
10. false

Minute 2
1. A
2. 9
3. 20
4. 80p
5. 3
6. 5
7. 21
8. 45
9. 10
10. 6

Minute 3
1. 1
2. 7
3. even
4. 7
5. 9
6. 8
7. true
8. false
9. 6
10. 10

Minute 4
1. circle
2. 4
3. 10
4. 3
5. 10
6. B
7. 11
8. 13
9. 11
10. 12

Minute 5
1. 5
2. Anna
3. 9
4. B
5. 1
6. 5
7. 15
8. 12, 7, 5
9. between
10. before

Minute 6
1. rectangle
2. 20
3. 8
4. 2
5. 8
6. 5
7. 11
8. 8
9. 7
10. 4

Minute 7
1. cylinder
2. 6
3. 5
4. 13
5. 3
6. 10, 6
7. 2
8. 4, 2 + 2 = 4
9. 10, 5 + 5 = 10
10. 14, 7 + 7 = 14

Minute 8
1. C
2. 8
3. B, D
4. True
5. 9
6. 7
7. 9
8. before
9. between
10. after

Minute 9
1. Tran
2. cube
3. 6
4. 18
5. 4
6. 15
7. 15
8. 16
9. 18
10. 17

Minute 10
1. $\overset{\bullet\quad\bullet}{CD}$
2. 8
3. 18
4. 50p
5. 12, 5
6. 4
7. Tony
8. soft drink
9. water
10. chocolate milk and apple juice

Minute 11
1. 6
2. 7, 9, 16, 20
3. 2
4. 14
5. 15, 7
6. 1 cm
7. Nancy
8. B
9. A
10. D

Minute 12
1. $\frac{1}{2}$
2. 10
3. 6
4. 13
5. 3
6. 5
7. 10
8. 20
9. yes
10. no

Minute 13
1. 9
2. 24, 32, 46
3. 20
4. 11, 3
5. 3 cm
6. 2, 2.15
7. 3
8. Puff
9. Floppy
10. Hoppy and Wiggles

Minute 14
1. 13
2. 12
3. 16
4. 321, 335, 776
5. 20p, 10p, 20p
6. 30
7. 20
8. 20
9. 30
10. 20

Minute 15
1. $\frac{2}{4}$ or $\frac{1}{2}$
2. 15
3. 2, 2
4. $\overset{\bullet\quad\bullet}{AB}$
5. 7
6. 10
7. even
8. 14
9. 3
10. 123

Minute 16
1. 9
2. 8
3. 0
4. L
5. 1000
6. 4, 4
7. 3, 3
8. <
9. >
10. 15

Minute 17
1. 9
2. 16
3. 5
4. 3
5. 75p
6. 22
7. 6, 6
8. 15
9. 30
10. 15

Minute 18
1. pentagon
2. $\frac{2}{8}$ or $\frac{1}{4}$
3. 12
4. 114, 142, 287
5. 10
6. 13, 9
7. 15
8. chocolate
9. strawberry
10. 3

Minute 19
1. £4
2. 308, 318, 350
3. g
4. 9
5. 20
6. 5, 5
7. 1
8. >
9. <
10. <

Minute 20
1. 7, 7
2. 8
3. 5
4. 42
5. 1
6. 27
7. 8
8. 42
9. B
10. C

Minute answer key

Minute 21
1. 9
2. 24, 42, 242, 420
3. 21
4. 4
5. 63
6. m
7. 2
8. 26
9. no
10. yes

Minute 22
1. $\frac{2}{6}$ or $\frac{1}{3}$
2. 3
3. 1
4. 4, 4
5. 43
6. 100
7. £4.50
8. 1000
9. 28
10. 47

Minute 23
1. 4
2. 7
3. 13, 8
4. 99
5. 9.35
6. 36, 42
7. 27
8. drive/carpool
9. skate
10. 10

Minute 24
1. 10
2. 50
3. $\frac{1}{4}$
4. 24
5. 5
6. 51
7. 7
8. 40
9. 30
10. 40

Minute 25
1. cylinder
2. 60
3. 0
4. 39
5. 70
6. 6
7. 24
8. 8, 5
9. 6
10. 25

Minute 26
1. 7
2. True
3. 6
4. 6, 6
5. 18
6. 101
7. 19, 91, 901, 910
8. 500, 9
9. 10
10. 20

Minute 27
1. 900 + 20 + 1
2. 2
3. $\frac{2}{8}$ or $\frac{1}{4}$
4. 12
5. £1.50
6. 3
7. 92
8. mL
9. no
10. yes

Minute 28
1. octagon
2. 100
3. 10
4. 4
5. True
6. 30
7. 92
8. cheese
9. chips
10. popcorn and fruit

Minute 29
1. 82
2. 500 + 50 + 6
3. True
4. 6
5. 14
6. 61
7. 2
8. kg
9. 30
10. 45

Minute 30
1. 8
2. 55
3. $\frac{4}{9}$
4. 30
5. True
6. 103
7. 800 + 30 + 1
8. 1
9. mm
10. 2

Minute 31
1. 16
2. 4.00 pm
3. 35
4. 8, 8
5. 7
6. 84
7. hr or h.
8. 4
9. B
10. B

Minute 32
1. $\frac{4}{12}$ or $\frac{1}{3}$
2. False
3. 9
4. 36
5. True
6. 4
7. 400 + 30 + 2
8. 62
9. 35
10. 9

Minute 33
1. 93
2. 48, 56
3. False
4. 6
5. 18
6. 11.05
7. 100
8. 4
9. sec.
10. 38

Minute 34
1. 15p
2. 72
3. True
4. 32
5. 20
6. 11
7. cm
8. 9
9. 210
10. 220

Minute 35
1. cube
2. 38
3. True
4. 36
5. 8
6. 10
7. 81
8. >
9. >
10. >

Minute 36
1. 54
2. 8
3. 5
4. £1.70
5. 91
6. 30, 40, 50
7. 49
8. watermelon
9. kiwi
10. oranges

Minute 37
1. 45
2. 1321
3. 9
4. 5
5. £2.75
6. 12, 21, 201, 210
7. 98
8. 12
9. no
10. yes

Minute 38
1. hexagon
2. 100 pence
3. 10
4. 64
5. 16 cm
6. 7
7. 3
8. 99
9. 35
10. 20

Minute 39
1. 18
2. True
3. 2
4. 389
5. 4
6. 2.15 pm, 4.15 pm, 6.45 pm
7. 36
8. 358
9. 30
10. 15

Minute 40
1. 21
2. 3
3. 27
4. 556
5. 8
6. 2 cm
7. 3
8. <
9. >
10. <

www.prim-ed.com   Prim-Ed Publishing®

Minute 41
1. 48
2. 5
3. 263
4. 4, 4
5. 65
6. 32
7. 486
8. 5
9. C
10. B

Minute 42
1. $\frac{2}{4}$ or $\frac{1}{2}$
2. 423
3. 64
4. 1000
5. 9
6. 6
7. 281
8. 35
9. <
10. <

Minute 43
1. 24
2. 48p
3. 54, 63
4. 7
5. 7
6. 12.00 or 12 o'clock
7. 545
8. 112
9. 8
10. *Amazing animals* and *Brain games*

Minute 44
1. 25p
2. 24
3. 883
4. True, 8
5. 4
6. 40
7. 6
8. 131
9. 310
10. 320

Minute 45
1. pyramid
2. 63
3. True
4. 7
5. 692
6. 48, 6
7. 28
8. 210
9. 40p
10. 3 cm

Minute 46
1. 36
2. 1433
3. 35, 7
4. False, 9
5. 207
6. £1.52
7. 564
8. 7
9. <
10. >

Minute 47
1. 56
2. 800, 60
3. 621
4. True
5. £4.50
6. 1
7. 148
8. 5
9. yes ⊂⊃ and/or ┈┈
10. yes ◇ and/or ⋯

Minute 48
1. octagon
2. True
3. 6
4. 2
5. grams
6. kilograms
7. 8 cm
8. 5p
9. 440
10. 76

Minute 49
1. £1.30
2. 270
3. 4
4. True, 8
5. 1
6. 8
7. 54
8. 542
9. 2, 0
10. 2, 20

Minute 50
1. 42
2. tonnes
3. kilograms
4. 69
5. 1 cm
6. 426
7. 7
8. 7
9. 2639
10. 322

Minute 51
1. 30
2. 440
3. 7
4. 5, 5
5. 15 kg
6. 4 t
7. 28
8. 105
9. 8
10. B

Minute 52
1. $\frac{3}{8}$
2. 5000, 50
3. 48
4. 50
5. 110 g
6. 5 t
7. 0
8. 759
9. 207
10. 6

Minute 53
1. 27
2. 40p
3. 42, 49
4. 877
5. 9
6. 5.45
7. 9 r 1
8. brownies
9. cake and biscuit
10. ice-cream

Minute 54
1. 50p
2. 40
3. 388
4. True, 12
5. 0
6. 600
7. 6 r 4
8. 36
9. 100
10. 200

Minute 55
1. sphere
2. 45
3. 24
4. 769
5. 7
6. 7
7. 181
8. <
9. =
10. =

Minute 56
1. 49
2. 7
3. 0
4. 6
5. 7000, 900
6. 457
7. 446
8. 2341
9. 359
10. 596

Minute 57
1. 72
2. 8000 + 300 + 10 + 1
3. 25
4. 30
5. £8.00
6. 328
7. 9
8. 308
9. yes ☽
10. yes ☺

Minute 58
1. pentagon
2. True
3. 35
4. 5p
5. 16
6. 7
7. 4, 2
8. 546
9. 634
10. 56

Minute 59
1. 48
2. £3.60
3. 98
4. 4
5. 7
6. 346
7. 0
8. 4 r 5
9. 7.15
10. 4.00

Minute 60
1. 36
2. 3 cm
3. 106
4. 4162
5. 703
6. 324
7. 6
8. >
9. >
10. <

Minute answer key

Minute 61
1. 490
2. 4
3. 126
4. 6, 6
5. 4 r 1
6. 46
7. <
8. >
9. A
10. C

Minute 62
1. $\frac{4}{8}$ or $\frac{1}{2}$
2. 3000, 4
3. 64
4. 5
5. 9
6. 18, 24
7. 91
8. <
9. >
10. >

Minute 63
1. 152
2. 12, 28
3. 70p
4. 5
5. 28
6. 3.55
7. 4
8. 15
9. 5
10. elephant and bear

Minute 64
1. £1.50
2. 336
3. 50
4. 40
5. 7 r 4
6. 8
7. 99
8. 300
9. 500
10. 300

Minute 65
1. cone
2. 7
3. 12
4. 4306
5. 9522
6. 12 kg
7. 3 g
8. 4 cm
9. 0.6
10. isosceles

Minute 66
1. £50.00
2. 4
3. 34, 30
4. 1
5. 8 r 2
6. 66
7. 641
8. =
9. >
10. <

Minute 67
1. 550 cm
2. 4000
3. 6
4. 89, 69
5. 2.55
6. £5.50
7. 69
8. 321
9. 679
10. 900

Minute 68
1. 90
2. False
3. 6
4. 5p
5. 16
6. 65
7. 16, 64
8. 349
9. grasshopper
10. less

Minute 69
1. rectangle
2. 4500
3. 44
4. 409
5. $\frac{5}{8}$
6. $\frac{3}{4}$
7. 3
8. 3314
9. 8.45
10. 2.45

Minute 70
1. 9
2. 8
3. 48
4. 2 cm
5. $\frac{3}{4}$
6. $\frac{1}{2}$
7. 150
8. 22 °C
9. Wednesday
10. 3 °C

Minute 71
1. 375
2. 8, 8
3. $\frac{2}{3}$
4. $\frac{1}{4}$
5. 8
6. 120, 140
7. >
8. <
9. C
10. B

Minute 72
1. $\frac{3}{5}$
2. 4000, 20
3. 1306
4. 5000
5. 6
6. 48
7. True
8. <
9. <
10. >

Minute 73
1. 128
2. 18, 30
3. 35p
4. 8
5. 1133
6. 1.40
7. 149, 158, 185, 194
8. lizards
9. 15
10. fish

Minute 74
1. 821
2. 5242
3. 6
4. 12
5. tens
6. hundreds
7. thousands
8. 500
9. 600
10. 100

Minute 75
1. oval
2. 1968
3. 72
4. $\frac{4}{6}$ or $\frac{2}{3}$
5. $\frac{3}{8}$
6. £1.50
7. 9
8. <
9. <
10. >

Minute 76
1. 2, 10
2. 7 r 2
3. 150
4. 6
5. thousands
6. ones
7. tens
8. =
9. <
10. <

Minute 77
1. 1, 30
2. 100 + 40 + 8
3. 88
4. 7
5. £4.00
6. C
7. C
8. D
9. yes
10. yes

Minute 78
1. 8387
2. True
3. 159
4. 5p
5. 30
6. 9, 7
7. 3482
8. game
9. 5
10. 4

Minute 79
1. triangle
2. 5
3. £1.00
4. 550
5. C
6. D
7. A
8. 230, 245
9. 5259
10. 3948

Minute 80
1. 422
2. 3
3. 5 cm
4. 240
5. ones
6. thousands
7. hundreds
8. True
9. False
10. True

www.prim-ed.com   Prim-Ed Publishing®

Minute answer key

Minute 81
1. 3, 3
2. 9
3. 186
4. 11.15 am
5. no
6. 5.45 pm
7. >
8. >
9. A
10. B

Minute 82
1. $\frac{1}{6}$
2. 4000, 800
3. 126
4. 2000
5. 4
6. 800 g
7. 1 kg
8. <
9. <
10. <

Minute 83
1. 4
2. 63, 81
3. 80p
4. 129
5. 7260
6. 11.05
7. 2000 + 500 + 70 + 8
8. 35
9. 5
10. Room 16

Minute 84
1. £10.20
2. 2
3. 7
4. 248
5. 5 g
6. 1300 kg
7. 1 g
8. 500
9. 290
10. 820

Minute 85
1. cube
2. 8 r 3
3. 72 mm²
4. 3148
5. 7063
6. 2999
7. 255
8. 6.55
9. 5 cm
10. £5.25

Minute 86
1. 11 871
2. 8
3. cylinder
4. no
5. yes
6. yes
7. 8
8. books
9. stamps
10. posters

Minute 87
1. 249
2. 2000 + 300 + 20 + 2
3. 263
4. 9
5. 9
6. 7365
7. 226
8. <
9. >
10. <

Minute 88
1. 75
2. 4252
3. 5p
4. 8489
5. 18
6. 9
7. 1000
8. 10
9. 60
10. 50

Minute 89
1. cone
2. 69
3. 9008
4. 45p
5. 30
6. 9
7. 6
8. 2207
9. 2, 15
10. 2, 20

Minute 90
1. 128
2. 9
3. 5568
4. 5
5. 7 r 6
6. 5265
7. 5201
8. blue
9. no
10. 6

Minute 91
1. 34
2. 6 r 3
3. 9
4. 5, 5
5. 3029
6. 4361
7. 6
8. $\frac{2}{3}$
9. A
10. D

Minute 92
1. $\frac{2}{6}$ or $\frac{1}{3}$
2. 5000 + 300 + 20 + 6
3. 135
4. 400
5. yes
6. no
7. yes
8. >
9. <
10. =

Minute 93
1. 4622
2. 75, 60, 45
3. 70p
4. 132
5. 7
6. 12.00
7. 6
8. 50 min
9. decrease
10. Friday and Saturday

Minute 94
1. £2.00
2. $\frac{3}{8}$
3. 27 m³
4. 96
5. 9
6. 1492
7. 3603
8. 450
9. 390
10. 300

Minute 95
1. pyramid
2. 5
3. 32 m²
4. 8
5. £5.50
6. 255
7. $\frac{5}{6}$
8. Ivy and Max
9. Ann
10. 3

Minute 96
1. 8
2. 72
3. 6
4. 6
5. 5
6. 12
7. $\frac{3}{8}$
8. <
9. =
10. =

Minute 97
1. £56.95
2. 4000 + 800 + 20 + 1
3. 5170
4. 93
5. 4
6. 8 r 5
7. 12 183
8. >
9. <
10. >

Minute 98
1. 4705
2. 7
3. 10p
4. 96
5. 25
6. 7
7. $\frac{4}{10}$
8. Sept.
9. 0
10. Jan., May, Dec.

Minute 99
1. 88
2. 8
3. 85 mm
4. 68
5. £4.00
6. $\frac{6}{10}$
7. $\frac{1}{2}$
8. $\frac{2}{5}$
9. 5, 15
10. 2, 10

Minute 100
1. 2196
2. 3150
3. 9
4. 84
5. 9 r 4
6. <
7. <
8. June
9. 2 cm
10. May and August